Minority Viewpoint: My Experience - as a Person of Color - With the American Justice System

By Sumi Mukherjee

Published by Crimson Sparrow

Crimson Sparrow
Livingston, Texas

Minority Viewpoint: My Experience – as a Person of Color – With the American Justice System

By: Sumi Mukherjee

Print Edition
* * * * *

Minority Viewpoint: My Experience – as a Person of Color – With the American Justice System

Published by Crimson Sparrow

ISBN: 978-1-946072-75-7

Minority Viewpoint

My Experience – As A Person of Color – With The American Justice System

"Experience is the most brutal of teachers but you learn, my God, do you learn" – CS Lewis

The following account is a gripping true story. Many of the names disclosed in this book are actual names of individuals, with the exception of pseudonyms used for Amanda, Kelsey, Mark, Mike, Gilroy, Jennifer and Barbara. All the actual names used in the book are in the Minnesota court case documents, readily available to the public, or can be derived easily from the names found in those documents.

Disclaimer

In this book I describe a true account story. I have given details on what actually happened, along with my thoughts, my feelings, and my opinions (only on this specific story) about individuals, systems, and organizations involved.

Most of the facts included in this story are supported by written documents associated with this case. But there are a few that were discussed with me verbally or were observed by me. I have tried my best to identify those facts as 'verbally communicated' or 'observed'.

My comments are not meant as generalized comments about the individuals, systems or organizations involved – my comments only reflect my opinions based solely on this specific story. My only intention is to communicate to the readers about what I experienced, what my opinions and conclusions are in this specific case, and what I learned from this case. Readers are encouraged to form their own opinions.

Dedication

To all fellow ethnic minorities, people of color and ordinary citizens forced to fight to protect themselves and their basic human rights and human dignity.

Table of Contents

In late May 2020, Vice President of a 13-member Minneapolis City Council, Andrea Jenkins, called for leaders to declare that racism is a "public health issue", following the brutal death of a black man named George Floyd at the hands of a white police officer while Floyd was handcuffed and restrained on the ground in police custody in Minneapolis.

Introduction

"There was so much I wish I would have known about our legal system before I became a part of it."

Let me begin by clearly stating for the record that I am NOT a lawyer or an individual with any proper legal training whatsoever. Rather, I am here to give you information from a harsh experience which many in the legal community may not want you to know before they pocket ALL your money. I am writing this book to save you from the misfortune I have endured!

Who I am is an ordinary person of color who has felt compelled to initiate legal action in two separate matters in an effort to bring about justice. The first was an employment law case in 2010-2011, which was resolved through an arbitration process facilitated by the union I belonged to. The second one detailed in this story revolves around Defamation of Character, commonly referred to as slander, occurring from 2016-2018.

In both cases, I learned a lot and suffered a lot, as the two concepts seemed to go hand in hand. Moreover, I always ended up SPENDING A LOT!!! Whether win or lose, each case left me with the realization that there was so much I wish I would have known about our legal system before I became a part of it.

It's one thing if the person bringing a lawsuit is rich and famous with endless means. But what about ordinary people like us who have our good names dragged through the mud? How are we supposed to restore our reputations if the system is rigged against us? And what about if you are not merely an ordinary person, but you are also a person of color? How might the various parts of the justice system and related processes treat you differently than they may treat someone else who was born with the gift of white privilege??

The purpose of this book is to help the next ordinary person faced with the daunting prospect of dealing with lawyers and/or filing a lawsuit. It provides a rare inside look into lawyers, lawsuits and the justice system.

This book also focuses on the epidemic of racism all across America today. It informs ALL ethnic minorities living in the United States – particularly fellow persons of color like myself - of the dangers we can face and how we can fight back without violence. We must never accept the indignities of being treated as second class citizens, as this story so well illustrates!

It is time to forget what you have read in the tabloids or seen a celebrity accomplish in court.

Through the sharing of my tragic, personal, true account story, I will educate the reader on what can be involved for average people and people of color.

Chapter One: A Hard Knock Life

"The greatest source of misfortune in my life is the fate of being treated as different."

No one ever promised that life was going to be fair or easy. On the same note, I also never dreamed it would be quite as full of obstacles and hardship as mine. The greatest source of misfortune in my life is the fate of being treated as different.

Ironically, it was the dream of giving their children a better life that had motivated my parents to immigrate in the mid-1960s to the United States from their native home of India. However, the so-called racial "melting pot" they had sought out in America did not live up to their ideals. Being raised in overwhelmingly white Minnesota in the 1980s and 90s, my younger brother and I were bullied and ostracized all our lives due to our being of a dark skinned ethnic minority group. We stood out as appearing 'different' in our community and were sadly treated as such.

Fortunately for my junior sibling, he excelled in academics and by his high school years, these talents had earned him a measure of clout with his peers. After graduation, he promptly moved away to California to pursue his post high school education. Ultimately he would stay in California, and found himself to be considerably less of a 'minority' living on the west coast with far greater racial diversity. He was also lucky enough to land a great job and be married at 30 years old – as it turned out – to a woman of the same race and color. He was also blessed in not having any mental health issues caused by bullying or anything else.

Not so much the case for me. As it does for many young people, the relentless bias-based bullying I endured took a much deeper toll on my life. By my mid-teens I had developed depression, post-traumatic stress disorder, and worst of all, an extremely debilitating form of obsessive-compulsive disorder. My crippling OCD symptoms soon dominated my existence and forced me to relive the years of harassment from my peers. I describe this complicated ordeal in my first book and autobiography titled *"A Life Interrupted: The Story Of My Battle With Bullying And Obsessive-Compulsive Disorder."* Speaking out enabled me to appreciate the prevalence of bullying, anxiety, and depression in our world.

To make a long story short, it wasn't until the year 2005 and age 29, that I began to reclaim my life from the grips of this devastating disease. Confronting the worst bully from my childhood – years later as an adult – was a crucial step in allowing me to let go of the pain in my past.

My 30s proved difficult as well. Bullying and OCD had effectively turned me away from the mainstream path of college, career, and family. Instead I took small jobs at hotels and volunteered with children in need. I tried diligently to have fun and make up for all the good years I had lost to my mental illness... from having had my life interrupted.

Romance remained elusive as it had since my high school days, with prospective partners in Minnesota admittedly turning away because of my race and color. Other times seemingly positive courtships would suddenly end without explanation. The relationships I did eventually have were full of stress and strange complications. Such was the case when I dated a woman and then had to rescue her children from a convicted child molester whom she fell in love with! I would go on to chronicle this shocking true story in my second book titled *"Father Figure: My Mission To Prevent Child Sexual Abuse."* Remarkably, I soon learned how disturbingly common such scenarios are which place children at a high risk for experiencing sexual misconduct.

Over time, my genuine love and affection for kids led me to a career in caring for children. Tragically, I came under fire in this line of work when I reported my immediate supervisor for her bullying and harassing behavior and her chronic mistreatment of the children in our care. The HR director, an even bigger bully than the supervisor, then fired me in an act of retaliation for my whistle-blowing! In this case my job was protected by an employee union, and my termination was in violation of the contract that existed between the employer and the employee union.

To combat my wrongful dismissal, I embarked on a year-long legal odyssey which included working with employment law attorneys, my employee union reps, and the state departments of human rights and human services. One year after my termination I would finally prevail in my battle and be awarded a financial settlement in lieu of regaining my job. I would go on to share this unique true story in my third book titled: *"How To Stand Up To Workplace Bullying And Take On An Unjust Employer."* This is a very important story since bullying and harassment in the workplace is a widespread occurrence in our country today.

With much help from my devoted parents, I officially began my career as a small time author and public speaker in 2011 at age 35. As I continued to speak and write books, I grew hopeful that traumatic events in my past were a long and forgotten occurrence. With time, I developed new meaningful friendships which helped fill the emptiness in my life.

As a matter of fact, it was an outing with close friends in late 2015 which would lead to my next legal fight...

Chapter Two: Negative Hotel Encounter

"Though my ex's mom had warned me that she felt there was a lot more racism in these small towns than here in the twin cities, I didn't really concern myself with what possibly lay ahead."

In September 2013, I began dating a lady who worked at a local restaurant in the twin cities (Minneapolis, Minnesota area) that I frequented. Although our courtship ended in January 2014, I became and remained extremely close with my ex's immediate and extended family members. While my ex proceeded to move away up north to Brainerd, MN, her mother and sister remained in Minneapolis and were local to me. As it turned out, my ex's three children also preferred to remain a part of my life. My ex's mom had informed me how deeply disappointed her grandchildren had been when the previous man who had broken up with their mother before me had failed to keep in contact with them, after promising that he would no matter what. Therefore, I was happy to stick around in their lives as long as they wanted me to. These youngsters primarily resided with their father up north in the small town of Crosby, MN with a population of about 2,300.

Sadly by the fall of 2015 tragedy had afflicted their family, as my ex's mom (who had become a good friend of mine by then) had been diagnosed with a form of leukemia in addition to other chronic ailments. Although my friend had intended to keep her diagnosis a secret from her grandkids to protect them, my ex's oldest daughter named Amanda had unwittingly learned the truth.

With Amanda devastated by the bad news, my friend (i.e., Amanda's grandmother) had requested that I travel up north and bring a mutual friend to help lift Amanda's spirits. The mutual friend was the teenage son of other close friends of mine and he was of Amanda's age. His name was Mark. I readily agreed to plan the visit and made a reservation to stay at the Country Inn Hotel in Deerwood, MN, where I had previously stayed once before. The tiny town of Deerwood had a population of about 500 residents, and was neighboring to Crosby.

In fact it was Amanda's closest friend from school at the time, a teen girl named Kelsey, who had originally recommended the hotel located a short distance from Kelsey's mother, Jennifer's home in Deerwood. Though my ex's mom had warned me that she felt there was a lot more racism in these small towns than here in the twin cities, I didn't really concern myself with what possibly lay ahead. Our goal was to help Amanda through a difficult time and that's where my focus remained.

On the evening of Friday, November 20, 2015, Mark and I made the two hour drive from the twin cities to the Country Inn Hotel in Deerwood. We arrived late in the evening, checked in without any issues and grabbed some fast food before getting to bed.

It was the next day, Saturday, November 21, 2015, when Mark and I met up with Amanda and Kelsey. Both girls had permission from their mothers (who had both known me well by then; Amanda's mother was my former girlfriend) to spend time with us that weekend, so Mark and I picked them up at Jennifer's home where Amanda had spent the night. The girls and Mark had been close friends since I had introduced them some time ago, and they considered me an uncle/father figure to all of them.

After some outings during the day, we all returned to the hotel that evening to swim at the pool. Amanda soon asked if I would be willing to allow four other local teen friends of hers to come join the four of us at the hotel for swimming. I said it would be fine for me to serve as an adult chaperone to all of them, and asked the front desk employee if there was an additional charge for non-hotel guests to use the pool for swimming.

It was specifically at this moment in time on Saturday that our evening took a turn for the worse. In fact, it marked the start of traumatic events that would affect my life significantly over the next couple of years!

Working at the front desk that night, was a heavyset Caucasian woman appearing to be in her late 40s with a mean and angry frown upon her face. When I approached and politely asked about fees for swimming, the lady rudely demanded that I must pay an additional $5.00 for each of the six teens to swim who were not registered guests at the hotel. I had no issue of course with paying the total $30.00 fee as required. (The six teens who were not registered guests consisted of Amanda, Kelsey, and their four other friends who lived locally)

What I did take issue with, was the manner in which this worker addressed me when we had spoken for the very first time – it seemed rather rude and unfriendly to me. For whatever possible reason, it appeared that she just didn't like me. ***

Having worked at the front desk of numerous hotels myself, I knew well that the golden rule in the hospitality business is that YOU MUST NEVER BE RUDE TO A GUEST! In fact it's well known by professionals throughout the hospitality industry that the customer/guest is to be treated like a king or a queen. Even if guests may routinely be rude to you, a good employee is expected to always turn the other cheek and remain poised and dignified. It is how they are professionally trained and paid to conduct themselves while on duty at work. This is true for a wide variety of other customer service jobs as well, but particularly so for those in the hotel business.

Here, at the Country Inn in Deerwood, an employee being somewhat rude to a guest – for no reason - really stood out to me! Regardless, we were doing this to boost Amanda's spirits and I was not going to allow this undesirable encounter to ruin our evening. I felt it was unprovoked rudeness but I decided to ignore it and we went about enjoying our time.

Shortly after this initial unpleasant encounter with the hotel employee, the four male teens Amanda had invited all arrived at the hotel driving their own vehicle. The driver was 16 and had a license, and it was my understanding through Amanda that these boys had their parents' permission to join us that evening.

Upon their arrival, we all took turns changing into our swimsuits in a lobby restroom located near the pool area. I would later learn that in the few minutes it took me to get changed in that lobby restroom, the teens had another run in with that same lady at the front desk. The kids would later tell me that the lady was interrogating them in a harsh tone about why they were in the lobby for even a few moments not accompanied by me, their adult chaperone.

She had also asked them who I was in relation to the teens, and they had replied to her that "he is like an uncle to us." If the lady had wanted further clarification as to how I was associated with the teenagers she could have asked me directly upon my return from the lobby restroom. She also could have asked me about this right when I had paid the $30.00 fee for all the kids to use the pool. But she failed to ever ask me at all. It appeared for some reason that she put greater credibility in what the juvenile teenagers told her about me, than in anything that I as their adult chaperone and her paying adult hotel guest might have to say. One has to wonder why this would be the case.

Once in our swimsuits, our large group settled into the pool and hot tub. Although it was a Saturday evening, our group made up the only people in the entire pool area. After about 45 minutes of laid back recreation, the kids began to get a little rowdy with one another. They began dumping water on each other's heads with empty recycling buckets and doing cannonball jumps into the pool. Being that we were the only group present and not disturbing others, I did not take issue with the carefree play the kids were now briefly enjoying.

But the lady working at the front desk certainly did. Out of nowhere, she suddenly burst into the pool area and yelled at the kids to stop their rowdy behavior. The kids immediately complied without any attitude or resistance that is typical of many teenagers. It's important to note that the lady made no initial attempt – whatsoever - to first address them in a polite or respectful tone like a dignified, well trained hospitality professional.

On the contrary, the lady then proceeded to also yell at me – her paying adult guest – for allowing the kids a little recreational freedom. "YOU ARE THE ADULT IN CHARGE! WHY ARE YOU ALLOWING THIS TO OCCUR??!!" the lady bellowed in a booming loud voice.

At this point I had had enough and I was not about to put up with this crap on Amanda's special weekend. Much like with the teens, the woman made no attempt to communicate her wishes to me respectfully, as both her job description and common decency would dictate. "Why are you shouting at me and acting like a brat?!", I yelled back at the lady. 'You don't get to talk to me in that tone! I AM YOUR PAYING CUSTOMER AND GUEST!!!! You speak to me with the respect I deserve or you leave me alone and back off!"

Without any prompting from me, all seven teenagers proceeded to clap their hands and cheer loudly as I firmly stood up for myself. I was shocked with how instantly they all did so with no preparation. They apparently could see how unusually hostile and out of line this hotel employee had been in her method of communicating with a customer. Looking furious and humiliated with a flushed red face, the lady stormed out of the pool area.

"Wow, Sumi, I've never seen you shout like that in the two years I've known you!" Amanda stated with great surprise. The teens then told me how this lady had hassled them when I had been in the lobby restroom. It was not as though I had left them unattended in the lobby for even a moderate period of time. They were teenagers and all old enough to look after themselves briefly. Obviously, I couldn't have brought them into the restroom with me while I was changing into my swimming trunks! Clearly this hotel employee had been spoiling for a fight with me upon our first interaction...for some unknown reason.

After leaving the pool, the teens and I headed to a local restaurant in the larger nearby town of Brainerd and had a late dinner. It was a 24 hours Perkins, and we stayed there until about one in the morning. Amanda then pleaded with me to allow all of us to return to the hotel and hang out in the room Mark and I were renting. While I would have concluded the night at this point under usual circumstances, I knew that Amanda was free for the time being from the thoughts of her grandmother's cancer. Therefore, I felt there was no harm in allowing the kids to hang out a little bit longer under my supervision. I knew we didn't visit too often and that this was a special occasion.

Upon returning to the hotel, we were pleased to note that a different and far more friendly employee had come on duty to work the overnight shift at the front desk. This employee appeared very well trained, courteous, professional, and accommodating, and it was a refreshing change from the antagonistic bullying we had experienced earlier in the evening. She was truly a sight for sore eyes!

Our group then proceeded to spend the next couple of hours hanging out in our hotel room. Mark had brought his Xbox along for the trip, and all the boys were huddled around him playing Xbox on one of the two double beds. Amanda and Kelsey sat next to one another on the other bed playing on their phones and trying without much success to distract the boys' attention. Meanwhile, I sat in a corner rocking chair and we all shared fun conversations.

Finally, around 4 in the morning, the teens were all tired and ready to conclude their night. While the four visiting males proceeded to drive a short distance home in their own vehicle, I drove Amanda and Kelsey two minutes from the hotel back to Jennifer's home, where the girls were spending the night. I then returned to the hotel and Mark and I slept in our separate beds.

Just as I was falling asleep, I received a text from Amanda thanking me for providing such a desperately needed enjoyable experience. Amanda shared with me that the other boys had recently texted her saying "Best night ever! Sumi is the most fun adult dude we have ever met!"

Chapter Three: Lengthy Complaint To The Owner

"Thanks for being a guest of my hotel. I can assure you that this will not happen in the future."

On the following morning of Sunday November 22, 2015, Mark and I checked out of the Country Inn Hotel in Deerwood by around noon as the rules required. Upon checking out, I inquired with the employee presently at the front desk as to the name of the lady who had been on duty the previous night. While this employee refused to give me the name of that particular lady, she did hand me a business card with the name and email address of the owner of this hotel. The name on the business card said Dan Brown.

Upon returning home to the twin cities, I sent the following email to Mr. Brown about our weekend.

Dear Dan Brown,

My name is Sumi Mukherjee and I am a 39 year old man. I'm an author and public speaker and reside in the twin cities (authorsumi.com). I have very close friends who live up north in your area, and I have been staying at your hotel whenever I venture out to visit.

Along with an earlier visit last year, I was just there for two nights this past weekend, paying $89 per night for Friday Nov. 20th and Sat. Nov. 21st. On Saturday evening, I had an extremely negative encounter with a remarkably unprofessional lady working the evening shift at your hotel. On this night, I had brought six kids who were non hotel guests to swim at the pool, along with me and another kid who was staying with me and was also a guest. As per requirement, I paid a total of $30.00, $5.00 for each of the six kids that were not registered guests, to use the pool. The lady was rude when initially asking me for payment. I tried to ignore her rudeness at first and to simply blow it off.

This get together was especially important for the kids I brought, as one of them had just learned that her grandmother is battling cancer. While in the pool area, a few of the kids began playfully dumping water on one another with a bucket near the pool. There was no one else in the pool area besides the kids in my group at this time.

At one point, the lady working the desk that night suddenly burst into the pool area and yelled loudly at the kids to stop this behavior, a demand to which they immediately complied. Then to my great shock, this lady proceeded to yell at me, very rudely, for my not having stopped their use of the bucket myself. It is of course appropriate for the lady to tell the kids to stop using the bucket, as they are minors and NOT paying themselves for any of the services being provided.

I, on the other hand, was paying $89 per night for two nights, plus an additional $30 for the kids to use the pool. Needless to say, the lady employee was completely out of line and highly unprofessional to speak to a paying hotel guest/customer in such a rude and disrespectful fashion! She could have made essentially the same point to me, but with the respect and dignity that she chose to leave out. Not acceptable behavior in the hospitality business!! I've worked in hotels myself before, and I was appalled and outraged at her insulting conduct towards her customer.

The kids refrained from using the bucket for the remainder of their time at the pool, and her choice to resort to such brazen rudeness was in no way warranted by the circumstances. A few of the kids then also informed me that this lady had interrogated them quite rudely earlier, apparently incorrectly believing that they were not accompanied by an adult (while they had been standing in the lobby) when I had briefly been using the lobby bathroom near the pool.

The employee on Sunday refused to provide the name of the very rude lady working on Saturday evening, Nov. 21st, but I'm sure you can determine the person's identity. I plan several more trips to your area over the course of the new year, and am quite hesitant to consider using your hotel in the future if this employee's egregious conduct is not properly addressed.

I would appreciate a timely response to my letter.

In turn, I was pleased to hear back from the hotel's owner within a day or two. The following was Dan Brown's email response back to me:

Sumi,
>
>Thanks for letting me know about your stay last weekend. It sounds like it
>did not go to well for you. I do apologize if any of my staff was out of
>line during your stay. I am currently traveling in Boston for the
>Thanksgiving break and I will address this issue with my staff when I return
>next week.

```
>
>I do thank you for your comments and will try
to educate my staff on issues
>like yours.
>
>Thanks for being a guest of my hotel.  I can
assure you that this will not happen in the
future.
>
>Sincerely,
Dan Brown.
```

Feeling somewhat satisfied with the response, I sent one more follow up of my feelings again to the hotel owner:

```
Hey thank you kindly sir for taking the time to
get back to me and for planning to address the
one staff member responsible for the egregious,
rude and offensive conduct on evening of Sat
Nov. 21. I would greatly appreciate that, as
I'm sure her behavior will turn away other
guests as well. Your hotel is a two minute
drive from my friend's home and I would prefer
to stay right there instead of at a hotel
somewhere in Brainerd. Hopefully this will not
happen again at your property.

Have a wonderful holiday and travel safe!
```

With these parting words, it was my intent to let the owner know that I – as his paying customer - had other options of where I could take my business if his employee chooses to behave so rudely again to her guest. I also wanted him to understand that it wasn't his staff in general that was at fault here; but rather just the one lady who had been working that Saturday evening. Everyone else had been quite courteous, accommodating, and professional just as I'd expect at a hotel. I certainly did not want all the wonderful staff to be lumped with the one whose behavior I felt was outrageously awful.

Following my lengthy complaint, I felt this negative encounter had been put to rest forever. I never thought I would find myself hassled by that lady again - and this time in a far more sinister way...

Chapter Four: Malicious Retaliation

"It was shortly after making and amending my hotel reservation in March 2016 that I began to hear disturbing reports about me coming from several of my friends living up north. Specifically, they informed me that they felt the local police in their towns were investigating me as a possible child molester!"

In the months following our November 2015 visit to the Country Inn Hotel in Deerwood, MN, I had all but forgotten what had seemingly been a minor bad experience with a certain employee. Amanda was doing well in her life, and her family seemed to be coping alright with her grandma's cancer diagnosis. Fortunately, grandma herself was doing quite well, as her cancer was in stage one and still too early to initiate treatment.

In mid-February 2016, Amanda informed me that one of her closest friends was being bullied at Crosby-Ironton High School, which was the high school up north that both she and her friend attended. Amanda requested me to contact her school and travel up north to give my routine presentation about bullying prevention, which was based on my first book and autobiography titled *"A Life Interrupted."*

I, of course agreed to do this, and contacted their school Principal who was very courteous and eager for me to come and make the presentation. It got organized fairly quickly and I gave the presentation at their school in late

February 2016. On this particular visit up north by myself, I stayed at a place in Crosby owned by Amanda's grandmother. After giving the talk I was able to spend a little bit of time in the evening with Amanda and Kelsey, who had both attended the presentation and had wanted to see me afterwards. Kelsey's mother Jennifer had specially come to attend my presentation as well.

As I would soon learn, this presentation was a huge success. The week after I visited the school, I received the following email from a student whom I had not previously known:

> Date: Feb 28, 2016, 9:24AM
>
> "Thank you for coming to our school last Friday at C-I. I believe most of us did learn a valuable lesson. I have been bullied by a group of girls at my school because I decided not to do basketball this year but do dance. Every time I would go into the locker rooms they would yell at me and call me a traitor. They stopped bullying me, and they stopped ignoring me. Now they even let me be a starter in volleyball. People have talked to them about bullying before, your story stopped everything, maybe we are not as best of friends as we used to, but now I am not being bullied. Thank you so much, now I can actually have fun without them following me and taunting me. Also other people in my grade have injured themselves because someone was bullying them, now those people who were bullied are actually happy for once. Now they don't treat each other differently because

they are different. You also influenced how people talk. Now at practice we banned the can't word, ugly word, and any other word that would hurt someone's feelings. I don't know how many times I can thank you. I hope you keep influencing peoples' lives."

Obviously, I am always thrilled whenever I receive amazing feedback such as this. It reinforces the very reason as to why I write books and share my true stories.
Sadly, my presentation at Crosby Ironton High School in February 2016 would also bring with it an unintended consequence. Little did I realize it at the time, but that employee who I had the altercation with at the Deerwood hotel had a young son who was also in attendance when I spoke at Crosby-Ironton High School. This seemingly innocuous fact would become highly relevant in the weeks to follow. ***

As mentioned before, I was able to spend a bit of time with Amanda and Kelsey in the evening following my speech. During our evening outing, the girls asked me if I would be willing to plan another fun trip in the near future, similar to the one back in November. It had been months since our last visit and they missed us. They requested that I again attempt to bring Mark and this time also Mark's younger brother, Mike, who had been interested in coming up to the Crosby/Deerwood area. As before, planning such a trip took a bit of time to coordinate with all the teens' parents and to determine their availability on the intended weekend dates in question. Eventually we all decided that the best weekend for everyone involved would be Friday March 11 to Sunday March 13, 2016.

Our decision made, I called the Country Inn Hotel in Deerwood and booked the new reservation dates. I initially informed the front desk worker who took my call that I would be staying in a room with two teenagers. Upon learning that Mark's younger brother Mike was engaged in another commitment and was no longer able to go, I called the hotel again and changed the details of my reservation from bringing two teenagers to now only bringing one... that being Mark just as we did the previous time in November 2015.

It was shortly after making and amending my hotel reservation in March 2016 that I began to hear disturbing reports about me coming from several of my friends living up north. Specifically, they informed me that they felt the local police in their towns were investigating me as a possible child molester! In fact, I was leaving a physical therapy appointment in the twin cities when I got the frantic call from teenager Kelsey. "Oh my God, Sumi! Sumi!! The police are looking for you! They kept calling my house and asking to talk to my mom about you!!", a shaken Kelsey relayed to me over the phone.

As if this wasn't shocking enough, I next heard from Amanda's grandma that Amanda's father was interviewed at his home in Crosby by a Deerwood police officer with regards to me. Confused and bewildered, I finally got hold of Kelsey's mom by phone and asked her if she knew anything about this.

And she certainly did. Jennifer informed me that a local police officer had approached her at home and asked her if she knew that I had been at the Country Inn Hotel back in November 2015 with a number of juveniles. Jennifer of course had been aware of the prior hotel visit, and she communicated to me that the nature of the officer's inquiries led her to believe that I was being investigated as a possible child molester!

As one might imagine, I was shocked, devastated, outraged and beside myself at hearing this disturbing news from my friends. Being thought of in the context of being a child molester was the worst false label I could possibly imagine. Even in prisons filled with all kinds of nasty criminals and murderers, child molesters are looked down upon the most by the rest of the prison population!

As our phone call continued, Jennifer informed me that the officer had revealed to her that "an unnamed employee at the hotel" had apparently notified the local police with a barrage of concerns about me in relation to the teenagers I had been with at the hotel way back in November 2015, now a full four months later. "I know who did this Sumi... it was that big, mean lady, the one you argued with at the pool!", is what Kelsey proceeded to tell me.

Remarkably enough, Kelsey herself had a history with this same Caucasian woman who I had argued with and then later reported at great length to the hotel's owner. Kelsey explained she had been acquainted with this woman through a babysitting arrangement several years ago. "I know her name Sumi!", Kelsey told me excitedly. "Her name is Lisa Vipperman. I'll bet she's the one who has done this to you now to get even for what happened in November."

Given the information available to me, I agreed with Kelsey's belief that this Lisa Vipperman was most certainly the individual who had reported me to the police. After all, who else at that hotel would have any reason or motive to suddenly now - a full four months after the fact – try to report me to the police for something frivolous from way back in November??

I recalled how the teenagers had cheered and applauded in November when I had argued with Vipperman at the pool, and the humiliation she appeared to have felt when that had occurred. I also recalled the lengthy complaint I had made to Vipperman's boss and owner of the hotel about what I felt was her terrible conduct as an employee. For all intents and purposes, it appeared I had been the victim of her malicious retaliation.

If so, then what had Lisa Vipperman said to make the police decide to investigate me??? It was a question for which I would need an answer as soon as I possibly could!

Chapter Five: Consulting My Trusted Attorney

"Don't be rude to anyone or look for trouble. If the police approach you just answer their questions truthfully and get hold of me when you can."

Ever since the employment law case I had gone through back in 2010-2011, I had become very well acquainted with a local twin cities attorney who I held in the highest of regards, at the time. His name was Brian Niemczyk with the Edina, MN law firm of Hellmuth & Johnson, and he seemed a rare exception in a legal world composed of heartless, cut throat, money hungry shysters.

Although he stood a good 6'5" inches tall, Brian was a soft spoken gentleman with a mild outward disposition. I respected him after the great job he had done in an unemployment benefits hearing I had against my employer during the summer of 2010. During that hearing Brian had been bold in cornering the former HR director who had wrongfully fired me. As a result, I prevailed in the unemployment benefits battle which later led to a successful union-led arbitration settlement against my former employer. In that case, I had a positive and satisfactory outcome.

Naturally, I had always kept Brian Niemczyk in mind if I had any legal concerns. Though very few attorneys ever could, he had earned my trust and admiration. We had kept in touch since 2010 and I considered him a friend to me. He'd invite me for lunch off and on through the years and we talked about our personal lives.

Following the information I received from my friends up north, I called my attorney Brian and explained the situation to him. Though I felt frustrated and wanted to confront the police officers about why they were investigating me, Brian strongly advised me not to do so. "If the police haven't bothered to contact you, it is not in your best interest to try and speak with them first", Brian told me. "Whatever you say can be twisted and potentially used against you, so I wouldn't recommend that", he went on to say. Instead, he advised that I continue with my plan to travel up north and to stay at that hotel as if nothing happened.

Brian also informed me that it might be of interest for me to - after returning from my weekend trip - send an official letter to the Deerwood police department asking for any reports with my name in them. Apparently, Minnesota law dictates that if such reports exist the police department must be willing to send the reports over to you if/when an investigation has been completed... that is if you ask for them. Access to the actual police report would allow me to see exactly what the previously unnamed 'hotel employee' had said about me to the police.

Still, I had fears about carrying on with my visit up north. These fears were compounded when Jennifer informed me that the police officer had asked her if she knew what time I would be arriving at the hotel! Regardless, Brian said he would be available by phone if necessary and recommended that I carry on with my scheduled activities. "Don't be rude to anyone or look for trouble", he advised me. If the police approach you just answer their questions truthfully and get hold of me when you can."

As it happened, Mark and I made the trip up north in March 2016 without being greeted at check in by law enforcement. In fact, we were never approached by any cops at any time. We met numerous adult and teenage friends over the weekend and did not run into that Lisa Vipperman character, either. What we did encounter, however, were some of the same local teens who had visited us for swimming during our stay back in November. Remarkably, I was stunned to learn from one such teen that the cops had also recently questioned *his* father about me! I kept this new fact in mind to report back to Brian upon coming home.

Unfortunately, whatever relief I might have felt upon returning from this trip on March 13 was short lived. On Monday, March 14, I was contacted through my author website by a man from up north named Gilroy, who identified himself as the father to teenager Kelsey. I didn't know a lot about Gilroy, but what I did know was quite negative in nature.

Along with the unspecified police investigation, Kelsey's allegedly scary, rude, and abusive father now wanted to speak to me...

Chapter Six: Dealing With Kelsey's Dad

"It seemed a huge coincidence that the police investigation up north and the sudden emergence of Kelsey's father both took place within a matter of days."

From the time I had first met Kelsey through Amanda, the teen had disclosed that she was not too fond of her dad. That is actually putting it rather mildly.

On the contrary, both Kelsey and her mom Jennifer had told me that Gilroy was allegedly a physically, mentally and verbally abusive husband and father. And when he wasn't doing that, according to them, he was largely absent from his children's lives. At that time, Jennifer was in the process of divorcing Gilroy for these and other reasons. I also knew that Gilroy had been arrested on January 10 of that year (2016) on a charge of domestic assault at Jennifer's Deerwood home allegedly committed against Jennifer!

It apparently had been quite a frightening scenario for Jennifer that particular evening. According to the Crow Wing County Court Administration report detailing the January 10, 2016 incident, Jennifer had contacted the Crow Wing County Sheriff's Office to report being in a physical altercation with her husband, Gilroy, and that Gilroy had allegedly cut himself with a knife but was saying that Jennifer had done it! According to the report, Gilroy had also contacted the Crow Wing County Sheriff's Office stating that he was cut by Jennifer. When a deputy arrived on the scene, the report states Gilroy admitted that he did have a verbal altercation and that he did push his wife to the floor.

Jennifer stated that Gilroy pushed her with two hands into the cupboards during an argument. She stated that she tried to get away from Gilroy when he tackled her and they both went to the floor. Jennifer stated she then went outside, Gilroy followed her and that is when she called 911. The incident concluded, according to the report, with Gilroy being placed under arrest and denying to provide a taped statement while Jennifer did provide one.

That case had been resolved when Gilroy pleaded guilty to reduced charges of disorderly conduct; thereby admitting to being offensive, abusive, noisy, and obscene. Along with Gilroy spending a night in jail, Jennifer said that she was granted an order of protection and that at the time, Gilroy had not been back in the household, except for by a police escort to get his personal belongings.

Though this was Gilroy's only documented arrest for abusing his wife, both Kelsey and Jennifer alleged it was far from the only time he had put his hands on his partner. Kelsey also claimed that her father had allegedly been physically abusive to her and her brothers when they were younger. This significantly impacted how she felt long-term about her dad, which she had expressed many times to me.

Soon after receiving the message from Gilroy, I was contacted by Amanda's grandma. She informed me that Gilroy had recently phoned Amanda's father and asked him all kinds of questions concerning me, for about an hour! It seemed a huge coincidence that the police investigation up north and the sudden emergence of Kelsey's father both took place within a matter of days.

My next move was to call Kelsey's mother and see if she knew anything about this. Jennifer said she had not heard from Gilroy recently. Apparently, Gilroy had been working out of state and had returned home three months ago back in December 2015. Jennifer informed me that she had told Gilroy back in December about my positive involvement in Kelsey's life and that she couldn't recall Gilroy having a major issue with it back then. It certainly appeared that things had changed now suddenly, for whatever possible reason.

Anticipating possible threats from Kelsey's dad, I requested both my father and my attorney Brian Niemczyk to sit in as witnesses when I established contact with Gilroy. This safety measure insured that if Gilroy lived up to his alleged reputation and threatened me in any way, I would have witnesses backing me up and I would be able to have him arrested. On Tuesday, March 15, 2016, I phoned Gilroy from my house and kept the call on speaker so my witnesses could hear it.

Although Gilroy was appreciative that I had returned his call, he took a tone which strongly indicated he was highly suspicious of the nature of my involvement as an adult male in his teen daughter's life. To set the record straight, I assured Gilroy that my relationship with Kelsey was that of an older friend and mentor. I expressed in no unclear terms there was nothing inappropriate whatsoever regarding my contact with his minor female child and that everything was always coordinated appropriately through Jennifer, who by now had come to know me very well.

I recapped for Gilroy how I had come to meet his daughter through my ex-girlfriend's child, Amanda. I explained how such meetings initially occurred when Amanda had brought Kelsey to stay at Amanda's grandma's home here in the twin cities. It was at such times that I would contact my close friends' teen son, Mark, and have him, his brother Mike, and their friend come hang out with Amanda and Kelsey to keep them company since they were all close in age and got along so remarkably well. Even though the girls lived up north and these teen boys lived in a separate far-away town, the kids all remained great friends and talked often via texting and social media. These three boys, just like Amanda and Kelsey, were good kids on the right path in life.

Sadly, Kelsey's dad failed to see anything positive from these interactions which very much brightened Amanda and Kelsey's lives (as per their continuous verbal feedback to me and to Amanda's grandmother). "Kelsey never had my permission to even be there in the twin cities!" Gilroy said to me in a raised voice during our call. It certainly seemed that I was caught up amidst the contentious relationship that existed between Kelsey's mother, Jennifer, Kelsey and her father, Gilroy. It was obvious the parents shared radically different beliefs about where Kelsey could go and what Kelsey was permitted to do.

But to my pleasant surprise, my call with Gilroy went far better than I had expected. At one point, Gilroy even told me that he felt as though I seemed like an educated individual. His parting words to me also seemed at least semi-friendly, as he casually remarked "Well, now you have my number Sumi, so save it in your phone." After what had been a shocking and stressful several days, I now breathed a big sigh of relief.

(Little did I realize it at the time that, sadly, this would be my one and only civil interaction ever with Kelsey's father Gilroy...)

Relieved for the moment or not, there were pressing questions that still needed answers. I needed to become aware of what Lisa Vipperman told the police.

Chapter Seven: Defamatory Statements Confirmed

"Any reasonable minded individual would've immediately reported a valid concern of this nature to the police right in November, no questions asked! They would not have waited four months! And they certainly would not have made things up in their report to law enforcement."

Following the call on March 15 with Kelsey's father, my lawyer Brian sent a letter to the police department in the small town of Deerwood, MN that had been investigating me for something. It took a while for them to respond, but over time we received a copy of the exact police report that was filed on Thursday, March 10, 2016, regarding me. The report designated the call as one regarding *"Information on suspicious activity."* Interestingly, the report had redacted the name of the actual person who disclosed the concerns to the police. It had also redacted the names of the juvenile teenagers that the reporting party had mentioned.

What the report did contain, were strong implications of sexual misconduct... allegedly committed by me. It stated that the caller was an employee of the Country Inn Hotel where I had made the recent reservation in March 2016. The report stated that the caller was very concerned about my visit from four months earlier back in November 2015. The report stated the caller was worried about "an out of town male being at the hotel with a number of juveniles."

The report indicated that the caller was concerned that the juveniles had been in my hotel room until four in the morning back in November 2015.

Remarkably, the caller had found it noteworthy to report to the police his or her concern that I had altered my March 2016 reservation from first bringing two teenagers to later bringing just one... as Mark's younger brother Mike had later decided that he wasn't able to attend. Why was a routine change in a customer's room reservation cause to notify the police?? Your guess is as good as mine.

But if the above mentioned information could be viewed as ambiguous to a devil's advocate, the following two statements in the report left little question as to the caller's true concerns and motives. The report went on to state that the caller was concerned that a specific local juvenile teenager - out of the entire group of minors - was likely THE ONE who would be staying in the hotel room with me during the upcoming March 2016 visit!

Though this teen's name was conveniently redacted from the report, I concluded the caller (presumably Lisa Vipperman) had told police it was one of the two female juveniles, meaning either Amanda or Kelsey, that the caller feared would be spending the night in my room. If correct, this would be a strong indicator of the presumption of sexual misconduct from the caller... allegedly being committed by me. It was a defamatory statement, as there was of course NEVER ANY PLAN FOR AMANDA OR KELSEY TO SPEND THE NIGHT IN THE ROOM WITH ME!!! The only one spending the night in the room with me – albeit in a separate double bed and with his parents' permission – was of course again Mark.

The second defamatory statement in the report, also attributed to the caller, was even more peculiar in nature. The caller had further gone on to truthfully mention to the police that I had recently spoken about bullying at the Crosby-Ironton High School. Somehow, the caller was aware of my presentation there at the school the previous month... and for some reason, had decided to include this particular fact in reporting to the police regarding this matter. Then in the very next line, the caller also stated to the police that I had been sexually abused as a child!

There it was. Right there in black and white on the police report. The caller had stated to police that "Mukherjee was also sexually abused as a child." This stunning, bizarre statement is 100 PERCENT UNTRUE!!! I was beside myself and astonished. I HAD NEVER BEEN SEXUALLY ABUSED AS A CHILD, nor at any point since my childhood!!!!!! But that's exactly what the police wrote down that the caller had reported to them.

At this point it was crystal clear to me what I believed had occurred. I felt certain that Lisa Vipperman had been the unnamed caller who reported me to the police. I also felt that she had done so as retaliation for our heated argument at the pool and my subsequent strong complaint to her boss about what I felt was her pitiful job performance.

After all, if Vipperman was genuinely concerned about a so-called 'out of town male being with juveniles' way back in November 2015, why had she only reported her supposed 'concerns' to the police after I booked a new reservation in March 2016?? The hotel had my home address, cell number, credit card info, and license plate number from when I first arrived in November. As a front desk employee of the hotel, Vipperman had ready access to all of that information. Any reasonable minded individual would've immediately reported a valid concern of this nature to the police right in November, no questions asked! They would not have waited four months!

And they certainly would not have made things up in their report to law enforcement. The salacious, untrue statements about a (presumably) female juvenile staying in my room and about me being sexually abused as a child were deliberately inserted to make me appear much more prone to being a sexual predator. Obviously, the thought of a juvenile female spending the night by herself in an adult male's hotel room screams sexual misconduct. And it is common knowledge and belief that many predators have a history of sexual abuse in their own childhood. Police, far more than the general public, are aware of that link in the criminal profile.

It was clear to me that Vipperman had calculated correctly that a report lacking these two specific defamatory statements would not have triggered a serious investigation of me by the local authorities. That is precisely why she had decided to make them up in her report to the cops, I believed. She had mentioned my speaking at the school to likely prompt the officers to show up there and ask around about me with regards to this 'investigation'. A police investigation of this nature would serve to discourage school officials from inviting me back as a guest speaker. What she did certainly appeared to be well planned out against me. She probably never thought in her wildest dreams that I'd read the police report!

Fortunately, my trusted attorney Brian Niemczyk of Hellmuth & Johnson fully agreed with my perceptions. After assessment of the situation, I gave Brian the go ahead to send a strongly worded CEASE AND DESIST letter to this Vipperman character. The letter spelled out our claim that Vipperman's statements about me to law enforcement were defamatory... meaning both untrue and harmful to my reputation. It also conveyed our willingness to pursue legal action against Vipperman if she did not reply and agree to CEASE AND DESIST from making more such defamatory statements.

In utilizing this strategic maneuver, Brian pointed out that if by chance Lisa Vipperman was NOT the person at the hotel who had made the report to the police, our letter mailed to her home address would give her fair opportunity to reply and explain so. "If we don't hear anything back, that's more evidence it was indeed

Vipperman who did it", my lawyer stated. There would be a cost for my lawyer to write and send out the CEASE AND DESIST letter to Vipperman, which I readily agreed to pay. And much as expected, we never did receive a reply to our letter which was mailed to Vipperman's home address in Ironton, MN, which is another tiny town near Crosby and Deerwood.

On a more positive note, however, I was very uplifted to learn from the same police report about the conversations officers had with both Amanda's father and Kelsey's mother, regarding my involvement with their kids. Both had strongly vouched for my excellent character when questioned by the police officers and said they had no issues or concerns whatsoever in knowing their children had been chaperoned by me at the hotel.

But if I thought that the matter had been put to rest, I was certainly wrong about that. Soon a fight between Kelsey and her allegedly short tempered dad would show how defamation had spread...

Chapter Eight: Evidence Of Reputational Harm

"I just got handcuffed by the cops. And they said you are a registered sex offender! Sumi are you?!"

Following the sending of our CEASE AND DESIST letter in the spring of 2016, life seemed to go on with little hint of what had occurred with Lisa Vipperman at the hotel. The kids in my life were all thriving and looking forward to their summer break.

Over Memorial Weekend in late May 2016, Amanda and Kelsey invited me yet again to bring Mark and his friends up north. This time, Mark's younger brother Mike would come along as well in addition to the other close friend of theirs. To avoid further drama in Deerwood, I booked a room at a hotel in the nearby larger town of Brainerd, MN. Along with my bringing two additional boys on this trip, Amanda and Kelsey brought two other female friends of theirs to join us as well. Once again, I was happy to chaperone the group.

While I was out having dinner with all the kids on one of those evenings, Kelsey received a text from her mom Jennifer, asking me to pick up some alcohol for Jennifer and apparently some adult friends of hers. Jennifer had texted Kelsey to request me to grab the drinks, as we were right there in Brainerd where most of the larger liquor stores were located. There were no big liquor stores near Jennifer's home back in Deerwood, which was 18 miles away.

Since I'd eventually be driving Kelsey and her girlfriends back to spend the night at Jennifer's in Deerwood, I felt good that I could spare Jennifer an unnecessary trip to Brainerd. Kelsey assured me that her mom texted that she would pay me back for buying the drinks, and I purchased the alcohol for Jennifer and didn't think anything of it. The rest of our visit that weekend went great.

However, on the evening after I returned home to the twin cities from this trip, Kelsey phoned me at 11pm with a startling confession. Guilt ridden, Kelsey proceeded to inform me that she and her young friends had intercepted the alcohol and *they* had drunk it *instead* of Jennifer!! This came as a big shock to me, as Kelsey had never before expressed any desire to try alcohol or for that matter to have me buy it for her (which of course I would have never done).

Kelsey validated my feelings of surprise and stated that it was one of her other girlfriends that was present on this visit - one whom I hadn't known well - who had come up with the whole idea for the girls to intercept and drink the alcohol intended for Jennifer.

Though I was initially upset with Kelsey, I quickly forgave her and told her that I appreciated her honesty in telling the truth about what happened. After all, had she not chosen to come clean to me on her own I never would have known what had taken place. I then immediately informed Kelsey's mom, Jennifer, as well as the mother of one of the other girls whom I knew, about what had occurred. I did so hoping they would understand that I had NOT purchased the alcoholic beverages with any intention whatsoever for the juvenile girls to drink them!

I also felt responsible, once Kelsey informed me, to relay the information to the involved parents so that they could warn their kids about the dangers of alcohol use at such a young age. It was my understanding that at least one of the girl's parents followed through with such a talk, and that girl later texted me and apologized tearfully for her role in intercepting the drinks. She acknowledged it had been wrong and that she had given in to peer pressure and gone against her own better judgment. She even said that she wasn't upset that I told her parents about it, as she felt I had done what was right.

Not everyone would share that belief. Regardless of my attempts to rectify the situation, in the following days, Kelsey's father Gilroy happened to communicate with this very girl's mother and thereby learned of the incident. Unknown to me at the time, Gilroy was furious and steadfastly decided that I had purchased the alcohol *intending* for his daughter to drink it! He was convinced in his belief of my guilt in spite of being told by the girl's mother what had actually occurred. (Both the girl and her mother would each separately confirm to me that the mother had explained to Gilroy what had truly transpired, but that Gilroy had anyway come to his own conclusion, regardless)

Gilroy's growing dislike for me would sadly reach its boiling point on the evening of Saturday, June 11, 2016. Tragically, it would intersect with the defamatory statements that Vipperman had made (as per the police report) about me back in March to the Deerwood police. This incident began when I was at a local restaurant in the twin cities celebrating the birthday of one of my friends who worked there as a server.

Around 10:30 PM that Saturday night, I received a call from Kelsey who said she was spending the weekend at her dad's home up north in Crosby. She was calling from the bedroom she slept in at her dad's place. Part of the reason Kelsey had called was to wish my friend here at the restaurant a happy birthday, as I had introduced them numerous times earlier when talking on facetime with Kelsey. *(Facetime is similar to Skyping where you can see one another's faces while you're talking on an iPhone.)* Suddenly during our call the line went dead and the call was disconnected. It was not uncommon for teenage Kelsey to suddenly end a call if she needed to go do something else and I didn't think anything of it.

That is until precisely 11:41 PM that night when I received a strange and shocking text from Kelsey. Still at the restaurant in the twin cities, I was stunned when Kelsey suddenly texted me from up north with the words "I just got hand cuffed! I'm not kidding!" Unsure if this was a joke, I texted her back "What happened and by whom???"

Kelsey replied texting me back "The cops and they said you are a registered sex offender! Sumi are you?!"

I didn't know what to make of this bizarre text message from Kelsey. As a teenager who liked to play pranks, I was hoping this was some kind of crazy joke she was attempting. But she wasn't joking this time around. Upon returning home, Kelsey called me again and this time we spoke on Facetime, looking at one another as we talked. Visibly shaken and tearful, Kelsey proceeded to tell me the horrible tale of what had occurred that evening.

Kelsey informed me that her father Gilroy had burst into the bedroom while we had been talking and demanded to know who she was on the phone with. When Kelsey panicked and didn't immediately reply, she claims the 6'4" Gilroy apparently laid on top of her and was squishing her to get her phone! That is how the line had gone dead when we were on the phone earlier in the evening.

Kelsey said that it then led to a physical altercation between father and daughter that escalated from the bedroom down the stairs and into the living room. Eventually, Kelsey said, she pushed Gilroy off her and into a wall. Kelsey's two teenage brothers and even her grandmother, Gilroy's mom, all became involved in the scuffle as well. At one point, according to Kelsey, her father and grandma had her up pinned against a wall until her brothers came to her aid and pulled them away. When one of Kelsey's brothers finally said "We need to call 911", she said Gilroy responded to that by snatching back control and saying, "No. I'm calling 911!"

And sure enough Gilroy made that call. Though Kelsey said she and one of her brothers were visibly distraught when the cops arrived, she told me Gilroy greeted them calmly and was the one to first explain HIS version of what had happened to them. Apparently, a total of six officers from Crosby and neighboring Deerwood had come rushing to this domestic disturbance call. When a frightened Kelsey attempted to slip out the back door, she said an officer cuffed her hands behind her back and sat her down in a chair.

And that's when, according to Kelsey, the real terror began. When asked by police who she had been on the phone with earlier, Kelsey told them truthfully that she had been talking with me, Sumi Mukherjee. To my shock and disbelief, Kelsey told me that two of the six officers then allegedly made the following several statements to her in her father's general presence, all concerning me:

- **We (police) know Mr. Mukherjee's name well from the Country Inn Hotel in Deerwood and have dealt with him in the past. He is a bad person and you shouldn't be talking to him.**
- **Mr. Mukherjee is a convicted and registered sex offender.**
- **Mr. Mukherjee flunked out of a treatment program for sexual offenders.**

- **Mr. Mukherjee we believe is linked to child sex trafficking.**
- **Mr. Mukherjee is dangerous and likes teenage girls just like you.**
- **Just because Mr. Mukherjee hasn't touched you during the years you have known him so far, does not mean he will not start touching you in the near future.**

I was flabbergasted and terrified upon hearing this information from Kelsey!!! When I pressed Kelsey as to whether she was telling the truth, she cried and swore up and down that she was indeed telling me the truth... word for word. I felt awful over how Kelsey had allegedly been abused and roughed up by her father! And the fact that the cops had all sided with Gilroy made her ordeal even worse.

After knowing Kelsey was safe back at her mom's and further confirming with Jennifer that this had indeed occurred, I looked up my own criminal record online to see if somehow a bunch of untrue charges or convictions mysteriously showed up in my records... but no, there weren't any such indications in my records. My criminal record online merely consisted - as it always had - of minor traffic and speeding violations. I knew very well that my records were clean, but because of these devastating statements communicated to me by Kelsey, I felt the need to go and check to be absolutely certain. Naturally, the police, more than anyone else, had the means to properly verify my criminal history, before making any of those alleged statements.

Believing Kelsey was telling the truth, WHY WERE SWORN PEACE OFFICERS OF THE LAW MAKING SUCH HORRENDOUS FALSE STATEMENTS ABOUT ME??!! I couldn't believe this was possible in the United States of America, here in the year 2016. I had always trusted the police and respected their authority. It was simply terrifying to fathom. I wondered if the officers had gained this absurd information when speaking with Lisa Vipperman? Where else or who else could it have come from? After all, the very first thing they had mentioned to Kelsey that night was my connection to the Deerwood hotel.***

Over the following days in June 2016 two more things would happen to further indicate evidence of reputational harm towards me in the small town community. The mother of one of Kelsey's young friends - the same girl who apologized for the drinking - said to me that she had been repeatedly harassed by Gilroy. The mother claimed Gilroy had been calling her and texting her and asking her to help him in his efforts to get me into trouble.

She reported to me that Gilroy apparently believed - from speaking with the Deerwood police - that I was a sexual predator and that Gilroy wanted her support against me. (This lady's information certainly appeared to further validate the alleged statements Kelsey said were recently made about me in her presence by the police.) The mother

50

claimed Gilroy was so persistent in his efforts to 'BRING SUMI DOWN' that she had to block him from being able to contact her! She also warned me not to travel up north anymore at all, as she feared for my physical safety with Gilroy nearby. That was quite an unsettling thing to be told, in addition to believing the police were on *Gilroy's* side!

And within five days of the June 11 police incident I would hear from Gilroy himself. On June 16, 2016, I received an email from Gilroy. Shockingly, Gilroy now stated in this email his apparent belief that I had disregarded his prior demand - supposedly made by him during our March 15 phone call - for me to cease all communications with Kelsey! He further claimed I had in turn showed "contempt" towards him and towards Kelsey, by not complying with his earlier demand.

As described earlier at the end of chapter six, Gilroy had in fact NOT made any such demand or request during that March 15 call which had generally gone well (fortunately, I had two witnesses listening to that entire phone call besides just myself to back me up on this fact).

Regardless, Gilroy now stated in this June 16 email a demand that I cease all communications with Kelsey... along with his willingness to pursue legal action against me if I did not comply.

Needless to say, reputational harm had occurred and I needed to act!

Chapter Nine: Deciding To File A Lawsuit

"This is a winnable case. I believe that we have a strong enough case to beat the Anti-SLAPP defense they are likely to raise."

The events of June 2016 had my head spinning in all directions. I felt violated, targeted, and unsafe like I never had before. Traumatized as I was, I knew that I had to act fast.

Unfortunately, no action would be occurring anytime soon. My greatest concern, multiple lawyers in the twin cities soon advised me, was to make certain that the small town police were not in the process of creating false charges against me. It was news of the alleged shocking statements that Kelsey said cops had made on June 11, 2016, which caused the attorneys I consulted to be fearful of this seemingly unusual and outrageous possibility!

While there was no way to be sure of this, both Brian and other lawyers recommended that I wait a few months before beginning a lawsuit against anyone. It would make hypothetical retaliation more difficult for the police, if a period of time had elapsed without me being near either one of those tiny towns of Deerwood and Crosby. It was terrifying – as a lifelong law abiding citizen – to imagine something like this could happen and to have to take precautions against it!

Impatient as I was, I decided to wait until August 2016 before filing any papers. The two month wait felt both long and excruciating. Though I felt the urge to take action against Gilroy and the police, I believed the true source of my problems was that same lady at the hotel. My lawyer Brian also assured me over several discussions that he felt I had a strong case against that lady, Lisa Vipperman. "This is a winnable case", my trusted attorney of six years had said strongly with utmost confidence. "I believe that we have a strong enough case to beat the Anti-SLAPP defense they are likely to raise."

Anti-SLAPP, Brian carefully explained, was a defense that all defendants in defamation lawsuits in Minnesota had available to them to try and dismiss a lawsuit if they could afford to pay for that particular defense. Brian predicted that if Vipperman had good legal representation, we would almost certainly expect her lawyers to bring an Anti-SLAPP motion early on to dismiss my lawsuit. **"The Anti-SLAPP is the big hurdle we will have to confront if we file this kind of a case", Brian firmly assured me.*****

Suing the Country Inn Hotel itself was out of the question, Brian believed, as I would need proof showing that the company already knew that their employee Vipperman could behave in the specific manner of defaming someone. However suing Lisa Vipperman as a person, Brian said, was something I could certainly do.

Brian also explained to me the concepts of defamation law in Minnesota, particularly with focus on a legal term he called defamation per se. Defamation per se, he said, occurs if you are wrongfully accused of a serious criminal act. The good thing about defamation per se, as I understood from Brian, is that you only have to show a false accusation was made *without* having to further demonstrate exactly how your reputation was harmed by the false accusation. Brian felt my case was definitely strong with regards to defamation per se.

Brian also went over other possible negative outcomes I may encounter; such as losing if a jury decided against me and the risk of drawing more public attention to the awful false accusations raised by Vipperman and others. There was also the financial aspect of the lawsuit to carefully consider.

While I certainly did not have the financial means to afford Brian on my own, my parents were willing to help me out as they firmly believed in this cause. As an author of a book about PREVENTING SEXUAL ABUSE OF CHILDREN, my professional reputation in this matter could not have been of greater importance! I felt as though my credibility and my career were both at stake, given the nature of the defamation that had occurred.

My father let Brian know that he was retired and we were extremely concerned about how much such a lawsuit could cost us. We then requested Brian to check with his management to see if the law firm Hellmuth & Johnson would be willing to help us on a contingency basis – that would mean we would not have to pay the legal fees as the case progressed – rather legal fees will be a percentage of the expected proceeds we would receive if we were able to win a financial settlement. Since Brian thought it was a winnable case, we felt the law firm would be willing to do it on a contingency basis.

However, after a few days, Brian sent me a letter informing us that his management decided against any kind of contingency arrangement. Apparently, they had big concerns about actually collecting any judgment we might obtain against Vipperman, in light of their strong belief that she was not independently wealthy. Brian also added that "we generally only take cases on a contingency when we are very sure of our ability to actually collect the money needed to pay our fees if we win".

In that same letter Brian mentioned again that "we (meaning him and his management) all believe you have a good claim and would be happy to pursue it on your behalf if you decide you would like to proceed". I felt encouraged with this last comment coming from him and his management about this being a good claim and made a decision to look at the possible financial impact for us. So we asked Brian to give us as good an estimate as possible regarding what it might cost us to pursue this case. Once again we made it clear to Brian that it was very important for us to know what it might cost so I could make an informed decision.

Brian then got back to us and told us that he estimated the cost of legal fees from the start of the case... all the

way through the end of an eventual trial... could reach around $60,000 in this matter. This was given to us verbally by Brian. ***

My father and I took a very good look at the financial implications. The case was extremely important for me since my reputation as a child advocate was on the line. We felt we could possibly handle the cost as long as it stayed under 100K. Since Brian came up with 60K as the estimate, we felt we could handle it even if Brian's estimate was off by 15-20%. So I mentioned to Brian that based on what I heard from him thus far in terms of this being a good claim and the estimated costs being around 60K, I was seriously thinking about pursuing the case.

Brian then sent me a letter on June 29, 2016, stating that he wanted us "to have the benefit of all relevant information about the potential risks and rewards of proceeding with a lawsuit" before I made my final decision. In that letter Brian reiterated the potential legal issues, including a lot of discussions on the possible Anti-SLAPP motion that could be brought forward by the defendant. Brian also elaborated on other potential practical issues that he had already mentioned to me earlier.

In this letter he also gave me a revised budget figure for a worst case scenario. He mentioned that "depending on how the case plays out, the cost may reach into the high five figures". I understood that Brian was telling me that the number could be anywhere from 60 to maybe 80 or

90K. But since we were thinking of a limit of under 100K, we thought we could handle what Brian was now suggesting. Since this was a very important case for me, I decided to move forward because in that same letter Brian also mentioned the following:

- "I am not suggesting that you have a bad case"
- "not to suggest that we could not overcome these issues, win the case, and achieve a satisfactory result"

Based on all the information given by Brian in this letter, I decided to give him my consent to move forward with the case. (**I later learned that there was more critical information which should have been included in this letter sent by Brian in June 2016 that I should have known about BEFORE making the decision to move forward!!!** I will discuss those key items later in the book.)

On Friday, August 26, 2016 at 6:45 PM, Lisa Vipperman was served in person at her home in Ironton, MN with official papers stating that she was "BEING SUED" by me. Though it seemed this day would mark the start of retribution for Vipperman, it turned out I had a lot to learn about what such a lawsuit involves...

Chapter Ten: Case Begins To Take Shape

"At the end of this lunch on Oct. 19, 2016, Brian once again assured me that he felt we had the winning hand in this matter. 'I'd rather have our case than to be on their side defending against our case!', my lawyer had stated."

The lawsuit papers which were served to Vipperman on 08/26/2016 also contained the complaint detailing my allegations against her. Under the law, Brian said that Vipperman would have twenty days to serve a written answer to our complaint. If she declined to respond to our complaint within twenty days, Vipperman risked losing the case without getting to present her side of the story. As good as that seemed upfront, I would soon be the one facing a setback.

Brian heard from Vipperman's lawyer on Tuesday, September 13, 2016, two days before the September 15 deadline. Brian was told that Vipperman wished to request an extension to the deadline, as she wanted to talk with her employer – Country Inn Hotel in Deerwood, MN - to see if their insurance company was willing to pay for her entire legal defense!

The defamatory acts we were alleging took place in the course of Vipperman's duty as an employee of that organization. Therefore, her private attorney advised her to ask if the hotel's insurance company would hire their own lawyers to defend her... all free of charge to her.

I was surprised and disheartened to learn that this was an option available to the defendant. It would have been great to know beforehand that there was a chance this could happen! It struck me as odd that Vipperman had waited almost the entire allotted 20-day period before making this request through her attorney, just two days before the deadline expired.

Instead of taking a hardline stance as my staunch advocate, my lawyer stunningly moved to grant Vipperman her extension to the deadline as requested! "Such extensions are granted all the time by the courts", Brian casually explained to me in defending his decision. "Besides, there may come a time in this lawsuit where we may need to extend a deadline of our own. And if that happens, they may grant us that courtesy then if we do this for them now." I guess I hadn't understood that the 'twenty day deadline' was easily subject to change.

Vipperman was soon granted not one but TWO deadline extensions by my lawyer Brian, who assured me that it "wouldn't diminish our case" if we did so. These generous delays gave Vipperman the opportunity to talk with her employer and gave her employer plenty of time to think and soundly weigh all their options. And sure enough, the hotel agreed to allow their insurance to pay for the defense. The insurance company then hired a top notch legal team to defend her!

In my opinion, this was clearly a missed opportunity for us. I believe that my lawyer should have denied the extensions (or at least denied the second extension) and instead pressured Vipperman to settle quickly. It's only after the fact that I thought that we had lost an opportunity. I now wish that Brian had focused on this opportunity. Brian knew very well that I was interested in getting to an early settlement of some sort. In fact he mentioned to me several times that cases of this nature typically settle quickly, out of court. A small sum would have been fine, so long as it came with a written apology and retraction of the defamatory statements she made to the police. I could have then taken her retraction and shown it to those police officers, to Gilroy, to staff at Crosby-Ironton High School and/or to anyone else in the community who may have heard the defamatory statements. That's what would have benefitted me the most.

The hotel being granted enough time to hire top lawyers to defend Vipperman – free of charge - obviously benefitted *her* the most! And besides Vipperman, it was also beneficial to ALL of the lawyers. The longer the case dragged on, the more money ALL the lawyers would be making... Brian included. Interestingly, it was me, whose name was being dragged through the mud in that community, who ended up being the loser out of this!

While Brian was quick to point out the advantage for me in possibly winning a large financial settlement from the hotel's insurance company (as opposed to winning a little money just from Vipperman herself), I WAS OUTRAGED to hear that the Country Inn Deerwood was defending their employee's wretched mistreatment of a customer! I simply couldn't fathom how any professional business which thrives on profits from the public would do this to a dedicated patron. Nor could I understand why they would do it.

They were supporting an employee who decided not to consult with any of her managers and instead went directly to the police to report an alleged "suspicious activity" four months later - with defamatory statements - to portray an unsuspecting hotel guest as a sexual predator!!!

I had put in an honest complaint to the hotel owner about what I felt was her rather unprofessional behavior. I had made it very clear in my complaint to owner Dan Brown that I had nothing against the hotel itself or any of their other employees. But the hotel still decided to provide insurance support to defend this employee. I was stunned to see that a hotel ignored the fact that a guest felt badly mistreated by their employee and had suffered great reputational harm as a result of their employee's actions!

In a real sense, this meant to me that Lisa Vipperman was off the hook; not only would she keep her job, but she would be given a defense far, far better than she could have afforded on her own. It also meant that she wouldn't have to worry about covering ANY LEGAL FEES WHATSOEVER in this entire lawsuit... thanks at least in part to the two allowed extensions.

That would certainly not be a luxury extended to my parents and me who were paying out of pocket! In fact, my folks and I had to take out loans and even dip into my parents' retirement to cover the rapidly mounting legal bills. People don't realize that every time you email or even speak with your attorney by phone, you are promptly billed for their time... unless of course your name is Lisa Vipperman and you're getting a full free ride.

On Wednesday, October 19, 2016, Brian and I met for lunch at a restaurant to discuss how the case was taking shape.

In Vipperman's reply to our complaint, her lawyers did not address or explain the reason why their client had waited FOUR MONTHS to report her alleged 'concerns' (about my November 2015 hotel visit) to law enforcement. However, they made the argument that she had not been acting out of vengeance or in 'bad faith' when she made the report to police about me in March 2016. They went on to claim that Vipperman had not been officially reprimanded by her employer whatsoever following my lengthy complaint about her... thereby implying that my complaint alone would not have given Vipperman sufficient reason to retaliate against me.

They further stated that Vipperman also DENIED making the statement to police about me having been sexually abused as a child (although the police report directly disputes their argument). Therefore, they argued, Vipperman had acted in good faith and her call to the police was covered by qualified privilege; which meant the right any person has to call the police with a genuine 'good faith' concern and not be sued for it.

One apparent big break for our side, Brain informed me, was the fact that Vipperman's lawyers would most likely not be bringing the highly anticipated Anti-SLAPP motion to try and dismiss my lawsuit early on. "I just can't figure out why they are not bringing the motion, but I'm certainly not gonna call and suggest it to them", Brian casually said with a chuckle. As it turned out, Anti-SLAPP would soon be ruled unconstitutional by the Minnesota Supreme Court two months later in December 2016. In retrospect, perhaps Vipperman's lawyers had gotten a heads up about this, Brian would later theorize.

(Very sadly, today I believe that the most likely reason they didn't bring the Anti-SLAPP motion was because there was an even simpler remedy available to them to dismiss my lawsuit... one which my lawyer mysteriously failed to warn me about, prior to starting the case. More on this will come later. ***)

At that meeting of October 19, Brian told me that he was concerned about all the depositions that Vipperman's lawyers were wanting to take in this lawsuit. A deposition is an official interview with a witness in the case which is conducted by lawyers with the witness testifying under oath and with a court reporter noting every word that is spoken. In a lawsuit such as this, depositions are taken during the Discovery Phase to gather information and

63

evidence which are later usable for any motion hearings and/or if the case proceeds to a jury trial.

Brian informed me that in our case, Vipperman's lawyers wanted to depose up to 15 people – including all seven teenagers who were at the hotel with me in November 2015! This was obviously something Lisa Vipperman could not have afforded to do had she been defending herself through a private attorney. Brian said the depositions, including one given by me and one given by Vipperman, would all take place between December 2016 and April 2017.

Brian also informed me that the depositions would largely take place up north in Deerwood where the defamation occurred; meaning I would have to make several long drives there and back from the twin cities if I wished to attend them in person. (As it turned out, there were 9 depositions and most of them took place in Deerwood, MN. None of this was surprising to me since if one reads the complaint carefully, it will be very clear that all these depositions were needed, to be able to figure out what was going on in this case. In fact, as we will discuss later, I believe Brian should have asked for 2 or 3 more depositions to make our case stronger. And it was also not surprising to me that most of these depositions would likely be in Deerwood, since most of the witnesses were from that area. I was starting to feel somewhat confused about Brian's concerns in this area.)

At the end of this lunch on October 19, 2016, Brian once again assured me that he felt we had the winning hand in this matter. "I'd rather have our case than to be on their side defending against our case!", my lawyer had stated. At that time I did feel like Brian knew what he was talking about, but later I would come to the conclusion that he likely did not know what was critical for us to win this case. There is more discussion on this in a later chapter.

Regardless, I would still need to learn and to understand what a deposition involved...

Chapter Eleven: The Art Of Being Deposed

"While a deposition may seem like a routine interview or conversation it is anything but either of those... rather it is warfare in action and can produce serious casualties."

As recently discussed, the start of the Discovery Phase of my lawsuit began in mid-October 2016. Though it seemed there was rarely a week that would pass without email exchanges between my lawyer and I concerning the case, there were three key actions that occurred over the next four months relating to discovery.

The first was the sending of a settlement proposal from Brian over to Vipperman's lawyers. This was our attempt to see if the other side was willing to settle the case early thus saving both sides from the ongoing expense of a prolonged legal battle. Though Brian had felt a quick settlement was very likely, there was no reply from Vipperman's attorneys to our settlement proposal.

I was obviously very interested in an early settlement. As mentioned earlier, all I was hoping for was to get some sort of an apology from Vipperman and retraction of the untrue comments she made to the police. It was a surprise that we never received an official response back from them. I asked Brian several times to check with the other side on this matter. He mostly came back with excuses from the defendant's side like someone was on vacation, or someone just did not have the time to look at this, etc. I was truly surprised because I thought insurance companies would typically try to settle things as quickly as possible – they could have gotten away with 5-10K instead of spending a ton of money for legal fees on their side. I am still surprised why they never sent a response back.

Again, I am left to wonder if it was Brian who was not able to make a convincing argument to the other side that this was a very good option for them, or was it just them not wanting to settle for whatever reasons? I also wonder if a heavyweight more-experienced lawyer might have been able to get this accomplished.

The second key action was Brian sending subpoenas (court orders) for any documents concerning me to both the hotel and the police department in the small town of Deerwood. Neither one said they had any relevant documents to hand over to us. Brian did not pursue this any further through extended court orders, as he could have chosen to do. At one time Brian had mentioned that he was likely going to the hotel with a court order for any and all related documents, but for some reasons he never followed through on this.

The third key action was the sending of two sets of interrogatories – meaning relevant questions about what happened in this case – one which was sent from Vipperman's lawyers to me and the other from my lawyer to Vipperman. Both Vipperman and I would have to answer all of the interrogatories and submit our answers to the other side's lawyers within a designated time period as mandated by the court.

In her answers, Vipperman finally admitted to being the person from the Country Inn Hotel who had called the police about me in March 2016. But interestingly, Vipperman now portrayed her 'true reason' for calling the police as concern for the kids being out past Deerwood city curfew in November 2015. She made this claim even though the word 'curfew' appears nowhere in the March 2016 police report! Also noteworthy, she now denied any concerns about sexual misconduct and again flatly DENIED having told the police that I was sexually abused as a child.

Like before, Vipperman's claims rang hollow to Brian and me. After all, we'd learned from the police report that officers began interviewing the teens' parents almost immediately upon taking the call from Vipperman on the afternoon of March 10, 2016. It didn't make sense that they were investigating a four month old "curfew" violation with such speed and urgency. Rather, it appeared they were investigating something far more serious, such as possible sexual abuse of minors at a hotel as insinuated by Lisa Vipperman.

Due to lengthy delays in responding from Vipperman's lawyers and the hotel's insurance people, these three key actions would drag on from October 2016 into January 2017. By mid-January 2017, I understood that there would be no settlement (since we had not received any official response to our settlement proposal from their side) and that Vipperman's lawyers were ready to begin scheduling depositions for this lawsuit. That meant that the fight was on and neither party was backing down!

As mentioned towards the end of chapter ten, depositions are done by the lawyers to gather evidence from witnesses that CAN and WILL be used much later for any motion hearings or for mediation or if the case goes to trial. Anyone with relevant information about the case can be sent a subpoena (court order) forcing them to give a deposition. Both Vipperman and I would most definitely be getting deposed whether we liked it or not. Vipperman would be deposed at length by my lawyer and I in turn would be deposed at length by hers.

What struck me as intimidating about the deposition process was the fact that it could consist of an interview lasting up to a maximum of seven hours in length! That's seven hours of sitting in a small room answering ANY and ALL questions hurled at you by the opposing side's lawyers. While a deposition may seem like a routine interview or conversation it is anything but either of those... rather it is warfare in action and can produce serious casualties.

If that sounds scary, that's frankly because it is! In a deposition, it's the opposing side's lawyer that is talking with you, not your own lawyer. And their specific intent throughout the deposition is to trick you into giving responses that bolster *their* case and that seriously damage *your* own case. They may speak nicely to you and smile but they are NOT your friend, as Brian specifically had warned me. Unlike a normal conversation, you must pause and think carefully before answering anything asked of you in a deposition. This is true most of all for the Plaintiff (the one suing) and for the Defendant (the one being sued), as they are the two sides at battle and with everything on the line. In my case, I was the Plaintiff and Vipperman the Defendant.

Prior to being deposed, the witness will be seated in a small room with both sides' lawyers present and with a court reporter who will type every last word that is spoken by anyone and everyone in the room. The witness will then be sworn in by the court reporter and asked to confirm the testimony they provide shall be the truth, the whole truth and nothing but the truth. The worst thing one can do in a deposition, I learned from Brian, is to lie or to say something under oath that can be used against them later at a trial.

Basically whatever questions you are asked in a deposition can also later be asked again in front of a jury. So if a witness says one thing to a question during the deposition and months later says something different to the same question at trial, the lawyers will be all too quick to point that difference out to the jury and to call the witness a liar. If you lose your credibility with the jury, you are much more likely to lose your case. It's really as simple as that.

Fortunately, through preparation from Brian and through my minimal prior life experiences with the legal system, I got to know well the above mentioned importance of a deposition. I was also glad knowing that I could ask for a break at any time during the deposition process, so long as I first answered the question just asked of me before I took my break.

Although Vipperman was deposed one day before me on March 6, 2017, I will talk more about her deposition in the next chapter. I was happy, however, to not be the one between the two of us who had to be deposed first. In effect, I gained the benefit of watching the ordeal play out with Vipperman one day before I had my own turn in the hot seat.

And a heck of a hot seat it sure was! On March 7, 2017, my mother's birthday, I was deposed at my lawyer's office by one of Vipperman's two lawyers. As her male lawyer carried out my four and a half hour long deposition, Vipperman's female lawyer sat in the room taking notes and staring me down with an incredibly menacing look upon her face. I believe her main purpose for being on the clock that day was to intimidate me. I was nervous but I tried not to let her affect me. Eventually I just shot her a smirk and deliberately looked away from her.

My deposition was very stressful and felt like being under attack, as fully expected. However I was prepared and overall did a good job. During those four and a half hours under the gun, Vipperman's lawyer did many different things to rattle me and shake up my case.

For example, he tried to portray me as a rich and famous individual; a so-called public figure. Of course I was and am just a small time author/public speaker with a minimal growing income. But Brian had warned me that it is harder for an established 'public figure' to show they were harmed by defamatory statements or that they deserve compensation for it. Therefore, it was the intention of Vipperman's lawyer to portray me as being such a big-time public figure. I made it clear that as much as I would love to be one, I was not in that category as of yet!

I also had to explain my lost business opportunity to Vipperman's lawyer in regards to speaking on a regular basis at Amanda's school as well as at many other schools up north. Due to the spreading of Vipperman's defamatory statements at the school and the safety risk of being in those towns with Gilroy and cops against me, I was never able to make any efforts to try to return there or to nearby schools as a guest speaker. This fact was important for the purposes of determining a financial settlement for me down the road in this lawsuit.

Next, Vipperman's lawyer attempted to use my second book against me. As you may recall from the first chapter, my second book is all about preventing sexual abuse of children based on a true story in which I worked tirelessly to save two young girls from a scenario which put them at a high risk for experiencing sexual abuse. Vipperman's lawyer kept trying to get me to say under oath that in my book I had encouraged readers to report *any* possible sexual abuse scenario to the police, regardless of the personal cost to the one reporting it. In this way, he was trying to make the point that in notifying the police in March 2016, Vipperman had merely done what I, myself as an author, was telling my readers to do.

During a break in my deposition, Brian reminded me to highlight the difference between someone genuinely reporting possible sexual abuse and someone like Vipperman who we firmly believe was trying to set me up. "Remember to convey that while you of course encourage people to report possible sexual abuse, that you wouldn't want them to wait four months to report it and you wouldn't encourage them to make things up if they report to the police", Brian stated. As explained, those are the very things that Lisa Vipperman had done, as per the police report.

In addition, Vipperman's lawyer questioned me extensively over my allowing the kids to remain at the hotel so late in November 2015; for my letting the older boys drive a short distance home around 4 AM after Deerwood city curfew; and for the unfortunate incident months later where the teens sneaked alcohol which I had bought for Kelsey's mom. Through his tone and demeanor, I felt her lawyer was blaming me for everything that had transpired. I, of course, responded properly once again to make it clear that everything was done with the knowledge and support of the responsible parents, as confirmed by the police report.

As you can certainly see, NONE OF THESE ISSUES were relevant to this lawsuit which concerns the defamatory statements made to police about me by Vipperman and the spreading of that false information and related notions through the small town community.

But in grilling me with questions over these issues, it was the lawyer's intention (based on my answers) to make me appear as an irresponsible adult chaperone if the case were to go to a jury. Regardless of what Vipperman *actually* did, if the jury believed I was a bad person they could be biased to rule against me. They could sympathize with Vipperman and her decision to call the police, regardless of her true motivations.

There were other moments also where Vipperman's lawyer attempted to bait me into getting frustrated and saying something that could jeopardize my case or make me appear vindictive in front of a jury. One example was when he asked me why I didn't sue Gilroy if I believed that he had spread false information about me. "I followed the advice of my lawyer", I replied.

Did you ever send a letter to the Deerwood Police Department and advise them that the information contained in their investigation report was not true?" the lawyer next asked me. "I was advised not to by my attorney", I again replied.

But Vipperman's lawyer wouldn't relent and continued to press me on this point. "You didn't contact the county

74

attorney and say, 'Hey, there is false information about me in this police report'"", he asked. "As I just said, I was advised not to", I replied yet a third time. "Because it would hurt your lawsuit?", the lawyer asked in a clearly provoking tone. "I was advised not to. I don't know what the reason was. I listened to what my lawyer advises", I calmly replied to him a fourth and final time.

At this point the lawyer backed off. He could see I was staying consistent and I wasn't taking his bait. The worst thing you can do is talk too much in a deposition. Your answers must be brief and to the point. You shouldn't volunteer more information to the lawyer of the person you are suing!

Regardless of having performed at what Brian would call a B+ grade level, the deposition was brutal and stressful... especially given my history of being bullied. Yet after a day or two I felt I was able to put it behind me. Difficult things do come in our lives. It definitely helps knowing properly just what to expect in advance.

But what could we expect from the other witnesses being deposed? Those crucial answers would slowly reveal themselves in the days to come...

Chapter Twelve: Other Witnesses Heard

"As one can see, Brian and I felt we had scored some big points supporting our case after Lisa Vipperman's deposition."

As it turned out, a total of nine people would ultimately be deposed under oath for this lawsuit, including me. Since I have already described my deposition ordeal in the last chapter, I will now discuss the depositions of the eight other witnesses involved in this case. While I attended each of these depositions as was my right being a primary party involved, Vipperman chose only to attend her own.

Even before Vipperman and I were deposed in early March 2017, the two police officers who took the March 10, 2016 report about me from Vipperman both had their depositions under oath on Wednesday, February 15, 2017. The names of these Deerwood officers were Ryan Franz and Mark Taylor. By the time of these depositions, Officer Taylor was the new Chief of Police for the city of Deerwood. We obtained the following relevant information from their two depositions:

- Both officers confirmed that Vipperman HAD INDEED made the disputed comment about me having supposedly been sexually abused as a child; Officer Franz asserted under oath that he recalled being "sure" of Vipperman making that specific statement to him and that his paperwork documenting it had indeed been accurate; Officer

Franz further acknowledged under questioning that Vipperman indeed stated that I was 'sexually abused' as a child as opposed to her having stated only that I was 'abused' as a child; Chief Taylor further vouched for the high accuracy of Officer Franz's written reports, as Taylor had served as Franz's immediate supervisor

- Officer Franz admitted he found Vipperman's sexual abuse comment relevant to the investigation of me because many predators were sexually abused themselves as children
- Officer Franz affirmed that Vipperman had expressed her concern to him that the juvenile female Kelsey would be the one staying in the room with me at the hotel in March 2016
- Officer Franz acknowledged he was indeed investigating me for possible sexual misconduct with the teenager(s) while Chief Taylor made no such acknowledgment
- Both officers said they went to Crosby-Ironton High School and asked around there about me, as Vipperman had disclosed in her March 2016 report that I had recently spoken at the school about bullying
- Both officers said they spoke to the police chiefs of Deerwood and Crosby about the investigation of me in this matter involving juveniles at the hotel in Deerwood
- Officer Franz said that he found it concerning that Vipperman waited four months to report to law

enforcement; Chief Taylor stated that an urgent
concern is typically reported to the police in a far
more timely fashion
- Both officers said they had in fact encountered
situations where someone reported to police
specifically to retaliate against someone else
- Chief Taylor said he felt no need to question me at
any point during the investigation, and he
confirmed the investigation of me was officially
closed after two weeks in March 2016 with **NO
FINDING OF ANY CRIME COMMITTED
WHATSOEVER**

Next to be deposed under oath, at the Country Inn
Deerwood on Monday March 6, 2017, was the nervous
defendant Lisa Vipperman herself! Along with
nervousness, Vipperman also displayed a defiant attitude
indicative of a person who appeared to believe the
proceedings were an annoyance and that she hadn't done
anything wrong. It's one thing to do wrong and to admit it.
I personally find it most appalling when someone either
lies, shows no remorse for past actions, or does both of
the above.

Interestingly, when Brian and I arrived at the Country Inn
Hotel in Deerwood for Vipperman's deposition, I found it
classy that the staff working at the front desk greeted us
quite warmly and generously offered us water and
refreshments. With so much of this book's focus on
Vipperman and the owners of the hotel and how I felt they

handled things rather poorly, it's noteworthy how the rest of the staff always treated me so well. It is certainly worth mentioning and a real shame that I couldn't have continued to bring my business to them for many more years to come.

We obtained the following relevant information from Vipperman's 2-hour and 32-minute deposition with my lawyer Brian:

- She down played the verbal altercation between us at the hotel pool but acknowledged seeing the full lengthy email complaint I had sent to her boss in November 2015; she claimed she was not disciplined over the incident I had reported to her boss, and said that she and her boss Dan Brown had actually laughed together about my complaint!

- She said she thought my complaint to her boss was ridiculous as she believed that she was only doing her job; she acknowledged it was the only complaint she had ever received and, more importantly, she acknowledged that she felt it was NOT justified

- She acknowledged she DID NOTHING FOR FOUR MONTHS to show concern or to investigate me and reported her supposed 'concerns' about me to NO ONE (not to kids' parents, police nor anyone else) between November 2015 and March 2016; she said she didn't dwell on my November 2015 visit after I left, and had moved on with her life; she even acknowledged she did NOT believe that a crime had been committed by me in November 2015!!!

- She claimed that she only looks at guest reservations that are arriving and leaving on the day she is working. She claimed she doesn't look ahead to see who is arriving in the near future nor look back. She couldn't give us a reason then why her supervisor Christine Yotter specifically informed her, days in advance, that I had made a new reservation to return soon in March 2016.

- When her supervisor (one of her two bosses, Christine Yotter) advised her in March 2016 that I would soon be returning to visit the hotel again, she claimed she had concerns about her responsibilities as an employee in handling my expected group of kids; yet most interestingly, she admitted she failed to consult either of her two bosses (Ms. Yotter or Mr. Brown) about those very 'responsibilities as an employee' as the most basic common sense would dictate she ought to do; she instead went alone to report me to the cops over my November 2015 visit without consulting her superiors; she testified she felt it was 'something I needed to do myself'; needless to say, concern over responsibilities as an employee in handling a group of kids does NOT correlate with telling police the specific defamatory statements they claim she said about me in her report!

- She repeatedly stated in her deposition that she was concerned about her responsibilities as the person on duty when there were 'unsupervised teenagers in the building' and/or when there were 'minor children that were not accompanied by their parent or guardian'; these statements were misrepresentations, as the minors were only left by themselves for the few moments when I stepped into the lobby restroom to change into my swimming trunks during which I obviously could not have brought them in with me; and I was there with them serving as their adult chaperone so it was not accurate for her to say they were there without a guardian; it appeared she intended to make it seem as though the minors were there without proper adult supervision which was NOT the case!

- She fully and completely DENIED making any statement to cops about me having been supposedly sexually abused as a child; her exact comments under oath on the issue were "I never made the statement that he was sexually abused as a child. How would I know that? I never made that statement."

- She herself couldn't recall during her deposition why she had felt it was important to tell the police that I had changed my hotel reservation in March 2016 from bringing two children to later bringing just one.

- She admitted that the juvenile female whose name she had specifically mentioned to police in regards to spending the night in my hotel room was indeed Kelsey; but she now claimed that she did so just because Kelsey's was the only name out of the seven teenagers at the hotel that she was previously familiar with; when specifically asked if she was concerned about Kelsey more than any of the other youths, she now stated in her deposition under oath "Not particularly. That's the child I knew." Regardless, she had no reason whatsoever to believe or to falsely tell police that she was concerned that Kelsey would be staying in the room with me in March 2016; Vipperman admitted in her deposition to speaking about me with Jo Olson, the friendly overnight coworker of hers who came on duty that Saturday night in November after Vipperman had left; Ms. Olson had seen me leaving with Amanda and Kelsey around 4AM to bring them back to Jennifer's home; and the following morning I checked out of the hotel again in front of hotel staff with Mark by my side and NOT with any juvenile female present; again, NO REASON for Vipperman to believe or falsely tell police that she was concerned that Kelsey would be staying in my room; she had no logical reason or evidence to support that completely made up, defamatory claim which strongly suggested sexual abuse of a juvenile female being committed by me; her deposition testimony on this issue detracted from what was in the police report and what Officer Franz recalled in his deposition about it!

- She claimed her only contact ever with Gilroy was when Gilroy supposedly came to the hotel and asked her questions about me in June 2016; aside from that one encounter, "I wouldn't know Gilroy from Adam", Vipperman remarked in her deposition.
- She couldn't explain to my lawyer how her attorneys had come into possession of a private email exchange between Gilroy and me; she claimed under oath she had no clue about how that had occurred
- She claimed that the very first time she learned that I had spoken about bullying at Crosby-Ironton

High School was from her son...and right when she was served with the lawsuit papers on August 26, 2016; however the March 2016 police report states that she told cops way back then that I had spoken at the school about bullying; a factor which both cops confirmed in their depositions had prompted them to go ask about me at the school during their investigation; point being, it appears she most certainly had learned about my speech from her son (or in some other manner) way back in the February/March 2016 time frame... as opposed to what she testified to under oath

As one can see, Brian and I felt we had scored some big points supporting our case after Lisa Vipperman's deposition. After all, she acknowledged knowing that I had reported her to her boss and said she felt my complaint criticizing her job performance was not justified. She acknowledged she did not believe I had committed a crime in Nov. 2015. She acknowledged having no concerns worth reporting to anyone about me until her supervisor tipped her off in March 2016 that I'd be returning to the hotel. She admitted she didn't bother consulting either of her two bosses at the hotel about her 'employee responsibilities' and instead reported me directly to the cops in March 2016 by her own volition. She admitted telling the cops she was afraid Kelsey would be staying in the room with me in March 2016 – though now she had walked it back in her deposition.

And greatest of all, she still adamantly DENIED the sexual abuse statement in sharp contrast to what the Deerwood police chief and a fellow officer had both testified to under oath.

Obviously there remained a huge discrepancy between the testimonies under oath of the two police officers and Lisa Vipperman with regards to the sexual abuse statement. Common sense illustrates that unlike Vipperman, neither law enforcement officer had a negative history with me nor was either one being sued by me, and therefore, it was most likely that neither one had any motive to lie under oath and commit perjury in the course of these legal proceedings.

There was a 2019 thriller/comedy film called "Knives Out", which features a woman who is prone to uncontrollable vomiting whenever she finds herself telling a lie. It is humorous to imagine how such a similar affliction might have affected Lisa Vipperman in the course of her deposition. I presume there might have been a considerable amount of vomit for her lawyer to mop up upon completion of her testimony!

I would very much like to publicly thank Officer Ryan Franz and Deerwood Police Chief Mark Taylor for their fair and unbiased investigation of me given the information provided to them in March 2016 and for – in all likelihood – telling the truth in their depositions just as they had been sworn to do.

It became clear to us that along with her confusing and contradictory statements, Vipperman's own testimony served to reinforce our firm belief that she had gone to the cops for revenge rather than out of alleged 'concern' for the juveniles with me at the hotel. As stated earlier, any individual in her employment position with valid concerns would have spoken to the police right in November 2015. They would not have waited four days, or even four hours... let alone the four months that Vipperman casually let elapse without feeling concerned!!!

Along with not contacting law enforcement in anything of a timely manner, Vipperman also acknowledged that at no time during those four months between my hotel visits did she bother to approach ANY of the juveniles' parents and inform them of my November stay! A genuinely concerned Vipperman could have easily contacted Kelsey's mother Jennifer (as we know from Kelsey and Vipperman that the two already knew one another) either during or right after my November visit and asked Jennifer if she had been aware that her daughter Kelsey was at the hotel in the company of an adult male from the twin cities.

"Did you know your daughter was (or currently is) here with other teens and some adult guy? Do you know who the adult guy accompanying your daughter is? Does she have your permission to be in his company at the hotel??" These were all valid questions that a GENUINELY concerned party would've asked Jennifer either during or soon after my November visit. If Vipperman claimed to not know the parents of the other juveniles up north, she could've learned their identities through speaking with

Jennifer. She could have spoken to ALL of their parents' right then as well...if she was actually concerned about the minors.

Vipperman could have even discussed this with her managers and if they all decided to check it out with the police, she could have done it RIGHT AT THAT TIME, without adding any other untrue statements and/or unnecessary comments.

However, none of the obvious common sense, aforementioned actions would have caused me to suffer reputational harm. That, in and of itself, is what this was *really* all about! That is why Brian and I believed that in March 2016 - when tipped off by her boss – Lisa Vipperman saw an opening for vengeance. She then provided her false report calculated to portray me as a sexual offender. And it proved effective.

Following my deposition the very next day on March 7, the next depositions in the case occurred on Tuesday March 28, 2017. These consisted of three depositions; those of Kelsey's father Gilroy, Kelsey's mother Jennifer and then young Kelsey herself.

Both Kelsey and Jennifer fully attested under oath to my great character and highly positive role in each of their lives. Both made it crystal clear to Vipperman's female lawyer that my friendship with Kelsey was in no way inappropriate, whatsoever. Jennifer's description of me consisted of the following: "He is a dear friend. He is a very polite man. He is someone that boys and children should look up to. From what I understand from his books – I saw him speak. I heard him speak at the Crosby High School last year, and what he went through and what he talks about – I think he's a good man."

When asked specifically about her feelings towards my friendship/mentoring relationship with her daughter Kelsey, Jennifer testified: "He is someone she can turn to and talk to. You know, sometimes you don't want to talk to your parents about boys or things that are going on at school, and Sumi is a sounding board for Kelsey." When asked about what kinds of things Kelsey and I discussed and if Jennifer approved of our friendship and communication, she said the following in her testimony: "He gives her advice on boys and dating. And, you know, I – sometimes I can hear their conversations or her side of the conversation, and there is nothing inappropriate or anything that they talk about."

When asked if Jennifer had 'any concerns whatsoever' about the relationship that I have with her daughter Kelsey, she replied: "None at all. They have a great friendship."

Vipperman's lawyer especially took issue with the testimony of Jennifer and baited her aggressively to try and get her to say *something* negative about me, which she didn't in spite of many harassing questions concerning my income, my mental health (OCD from my past) and the nature of my contact via phone calls and texts with Kelsey.

It seemed any tactic this lawyer had up her sleeve was fair game!

The lawyer also hammered Jennifer with questions regarding the notorious alcohol incident in May 2016 as well as other incidents involving their family which also had nothing to do with my case. In her deposition, Jennifer was crystal clear about what had actually occurred regarding the alcohol. When asked about what Kelsey had said to Jennifer about how she got alcohol and what the circumstances were of her drinking, Jennifer replied "Just that she – Sumi had bought them for me at my request and that, when I – when they arrived home and I was sleeping, they decided to drink them."

Jennifer further described the reaction of the one of the other girls' mothers... that being the one who had spoken to me about being hassled by Gilroy. When asked if that mother blamed me for the girls drinking the alcohol, Jennifer replied "No." When further asked what was specifically said between them about it, Jennifer replied "I told her that the alcohol was bought for me and that the girls chose to drink it." Jennifer said that the other mother responded by saying, "That really does not surprise me. They are teenage girls."

Eventually, the two would butt heads hard when Vipperman's lawyer asked, for what seemed like the tenth time, if Jennifer had any concerns about the nature of my friendship with Kelsey.

"I pride myself on being a good judge of character, and I'm totally fine with Sumi hanging out with my daughter. I will say that till the day I die!" Jennifer said with exasperation to the much repeated question. "Well good, I'm glad you're happy with that", Vipperman's lawyer shot back at the mother unexpectedly with a snotty attitude. "Objection, argumentative!" my lawyer Brian finally spoke up. "And sarcastic!" Jennifer added with frustration.

Though she was significantly gentler when questioning Kelsey, Vipperman's lawyer tried hard to confuse the teen about exactly what she recalled those officers had allegedly said about me – word for word - at her dad's home back in June 2016. While Kelsey recalled most of the alleged cop statements she had relayed to me back at that time, Vipperman's lawyer was able to trick the teen into also agreeing she had heard the officers saying other random things which the sly attorney was making up right on the spot! It was the lawyer's intent to portray Kelsey as an immature kid who was prone to stretching the truth and therefore wasn't trustworthy in anything she was saying.

The lawyer also peppered Kelsey with questions about the nature of her friendship and regular contact with me. "Do you have feelings for Sumi like you would for a boyfriend?", the lawyer had the audacity to ask the stunned 15-year old female child. "No, we are good friends, GOOD FRIENDS!", a taken back Kelsey replied. **(Jennifer would tell me just how shocked and appalled** her daughter felt at this lawyer's nasty insinuation that our mentoring/friendship could possibly be inappropriate in any way, shape, or form. "She told me that question made her stomach turn", Jennifer would tell me later that same day when I called to check and see how Kelsey was doing after her hour-long deposition.)

"He is a big part of my life", the teen continued. "Somebody that I can always rely on to help me through whatever I'm going through." It was aggravating, difficult and stressful to sit and watch my close friends struggle through this prolonged ordeal. I hadn't understood that my filing a lawsuit could lead to this kind of distress... for myself as well as for others!!!

But young Kelsey did incredibly well, especially for someone having to give a deposition in a lawsuit at her tender age. She was forthcoming in her answers concerning several issues including those about her father's outspoken hatred for me... attributing it to jealousy. "But do you think maybe some part of your dad is just being the protective dad for his baby?", Vipperman's lawyer suggested coaxingly to the teenager. "No", Kelsey replied firmly with confidence... "Because my mom has mentioned to him numerous times who Sumi is. He's just jealous because I have a better relationship with Sumi than I do with him. My dad's not in my life really."

Kelsey's father, Gilroy, in turn shifted between being rude, defiant and forgetful of key events during his three hours long deposition earlier that same morning. It was interesting to meet this individual for the first time after everything I had heard about him from Kelsey and Jennifer. Sadly, I could see how short tempered Gilroy could be and how the slightest question here or there would suddenly set him off. There were several instances when Gilroy became loud and full of rage while discussing certain aspects of this matter.

Gilroy's temper became a serious issue when Vipperman's lawyer revealed to him that I had still maintained some communications with Kelsey following his threatening email in June 2016 ordering me to not do so. (I had revealed this during my deposition when specifically asked by Vipperman's lawyer if I still communicate with Kelsey. Brian and I had purposefully selected city hall near the Deerwood police department for the setting of Gilroy's deposition, should Gilroy once again choose to escalate his behavior towards a charge of disorderly conduct.)

What the lawyer didn't bother to explain for Gilroy was the fact that I had indeed stopped communicating with Kelsey after receiving Gilroy's June 2016 email and months later resumed some communications ONLY after much pleading from Kelsey and then also ONLY with full consent and approval from Jennifer who was the primary custodial parent and with whom Kelsey resided.

Still, if Vipperman's lawyer leaked this information intending to cause a big stir, Gilroy didn't disappoint her. Gilroy stared me down and hollered at me with a look of pure hate upon his scowling face. "YOU KEEP YOUR

GODDAMN MITTS AWAY FROM MY DAUGHTER!!!!! DON'T YOU UNDERSTAND ENGLISH?!?!" he furiously bellowed.

At this point, my lawyer had to intervene and told Gilroy "this is not the time to shout at my client. Your job here is to answer our questions and that is all." Sitting in that small room facing him, I could only imagine what Kelsey and Jennifer had allegedly endured spending years on the receiving end of Gilroy's violent rage. I had heard that for the two of them, it had not merely been limited to the verbal abuse that I was now experiencing. I marveled at what courage it had taken for Jennifer to finally have him arrested and held accountable under the law, and then to emancipate herself from years of abuse by divorcing him.

In fact during her deposition later that same afternoon, Jennifer would go on to state the following regarding her marriage to Gilroy, "There was a lot of mental, physical and verbal abuse that I had taken for many years. If you ever voiced your opinion or your thoughts on any subject out there with Gilroy, if it's not the same as his, it doesn't matter, and he can get very loud and verbal and scary."

For my part, it was very difficult to just sit there and not be able to respond or explain myself. But I knew that engaging in any verbal altercation at this moment could harm my case. While the loud and obnoxious Gilroy had nothing to lose, I knew the court reporter was typing out every last word being spoken.

Any verbal altercation with Gilroy (if I were to respond), could be read in front of a jury in court by Vipperman's lawyer. And of course, such an altercation could then be used by Vipperman's lawyer to cast me in a negative light. If Vipperman's lawyer was hoping that I would take the bait, I was glad to disappoint her on that. Instead, I looked away as Gilroy's ranting and raving eventually calmed to a menacing stare.

Despite his abusive demeanor, Gilroy did provide some useful information to Brian and me for our lawsuit. He informed us that he had first learned of my November 2015 hotel visit from one of the officers who had come to his home on June 11, 2016. His contact with that officer, a Deerwood cop named Damien Stalker, prompted Gilroy to visit the hotel in person the following week where he ran into none other than Lisa Vipperman, the defendant herself!

Gilroy said Vipperman informed him that she had indeed called the police over my visit to the hotel in which his daughter was present and allegedly involved in an incident. "MY TEENAGE DAUGHTER SHOULD NOT BE HAVING 'INCIDENTS' AT HOTELS!!!", Gilroy roared at me during his deposition. According to Gilroy's testimony, Vipperman's use of the term incident had left Gilroy believing something terrible had happened.

It was clear to me that it was all part of the Vipperman strategy aimed to make people fear and despise me. And it was working! Gilroy, like most average people, assumed that if the police were called over an "incident" that it must have been something pretty serious. He also likely took for granted that the information Vipperman provided to the police had been truthful and accurate... which it is in most cases where people call the police. This was likely the same thought process of officials at Crosby-Ironton High School. None of them could have known at that time what the evidence shows us today; that this was a vindictive act of a person who wanted me out of her town!

Testifying that he was still confused about what had actually transpired (with the kids at the hotel) following his meeting with Vipperman, Gilroy said he then spoke to the person who had been the chief of police of Deerwood, back in June 2016. Gilroy stated this former chief's name was Harry Gottsch. When specifically asked what he remembered about his conversation with Chief Gottsch, Gilroy made the following claim under oath during his deposition, "Chief Gottsch said that the actions that were going on there (at the hotel) were – he would have the same concerns that I do that there was – they were predatory!"

If actually true, this was stunning to Brian and me. According to Gilroy's testimony, Chief Gottsch did not bother to simply inform Gilroy in June 2016 that the 'investigation' of me had concluded way back in March 2016 with **NO FINDING OF ANY WRONGDOING!!!!!!!!** So much for my being vindicated, I guess. Right there is the encompassing power of defamatory statements and implications - especially with regards to false allegations involving mistreatment of minors. Whether fully disproven or not, they leave doubt in a person's mind and a stain that cannot be removed.

It was clear for Brian and me to see how defamatory statements had spread and what influence they carried in this small town community. Gilroy also admitted relaying his beliefs about me to another parent in the area, and further revealed that he had reported me to law enforcement multiple times over the May 2016 alcohol incident. Those police officers who he had reported me to never took action against me for obvious reasons. Both Kelsey and her mom told the cops truthfully that I was unaware of the teenagers' deceptive plans to intercept the mom's alcohol. I was never charged or even questioned by officers regarding that unfortunate matter.

Finally, the last two witnesses to be deposed were the police officers who Kelsey alleged had made the series of absurd, defamatory statements about me (discussed earlier in chapter eight) on June 11, 2016. They were officers Brandon Nadeau and Damien Stalker. Their depositions took place in two different towns on Monday April 17, 2017.

Interestingly, Officer Stalker informed us that he had remembered my unique name just from briefly viewing Vipperman's report in March 2016 at the Deerwood police department. "Because it's a name that I don't -- I -- I wouldn't really forget it. It's the only name I've ever seen like that, so I recalled it. And I recalled that there were -- again, I recalled -- all I knew from that prior incident was just something involving juveniles at the hotel", Officer Stalker stated during his deposition.

When Gilroy told Officer Stalker on June 11, 2016 that his daughter had been speaking with a 'Sumi Mukherjee', Officer Stalker recalled my name and then told Gilroy he had known of me from the prior hotel incident involving juveniles. Right there was the connection of Vipperman's statements to the incident months later with Gilroy and Kelsey! During his deposition officer Stalker commented, "When dad says 'he's providing alcohol to my juvenile daughter in a hotel room', and I recently saw an incident report with his name and then a bunch of juveniles, CLICK. That's where I got the impression we were dealing with the same individual."

Incredibly, Officer Stalker testified that Gilroy informed him that I had been serving alcoholic beverages to Kelsey and her juvenile friends inside hotel rooms. According to Stalker's testimony, it was clear that Gilroy had completely misstated and misrepresented what had actually transpired. When asked in his deposition what Gilroy had said to him about my contact with Kelsey, Officer Stalker replied, "Just what the father had told me and the other officers, that he was upset because he believed that the other party that his daughter was talking to was furnishing her alcohol in hotel rooms."

As explained before, I purchased alcohol intended ONLY for Jennifer at Jennifer's request. It was much later that same evening, once I was no longer there at Jennifer's residence in Deerwood, that the girls had sneaked some of Jennifer's drinks while she slept, as per their intended plan and Jennifer's deposition testimony. NO JUVENILE WAS SERVED ALCOHOL BY ME INSIDE ANY HOTEL ROOM!!!!!!!!! It was nothing less than outrageous and defamatory how Gilroy was lying about this to police (as per Officer Stalker's testimony) – whether intentionally or through some sort of severe misunderstanding.

Officer Stalker also testified that he hadn't known - when informing Gilroy in June 2016 – that the investigation of me had been closed way back in March 2016 with **NO FINDING OF ANY WRONGDOING**. As we heard earlier from Gilroy, it was *this* officer's recollection of Vipperman's report that prompted Gilroy to visit the hotel and speak to Vipperman in person. In other words, Vipperman's defamatory comments from March had taken on a life of their own! It was only after learning about the hotel that Gilroy asked me not to communicate with Kelsey.

While officers Nadeau and Stalker both firmly denied making the exact series of absurd, defamatory statements which Kelsey alleged back in chapter eight, Officer Stalker did admit that the cops had been advocating on Gilroy's behalf that evening when they arrived on scene, just as Kelsey told me they had. "I told her, and I believe the

97

other officers did as well. We told her -- we gave her kind of a vague generalization of Internet online predators. We -- we kind of summed it up. It was more of a scare tactic to kind of get her to understand our view, because we were fighting on dad's side at that time", Officer Stalker stated in his deposition.

Also in regards to his comments to Kelsey that night, Officer Stalker said the following in his deposition: "It was a vague kind of generalized, hypothetical-type speech. I don't remember the exact wording. I don't." Officer Stalker further stated the following on this subject: "I can't remember every word that we exchanged between the two of us in that time period. I just know, in general, that was what was discussed. I gave her some hypotheticals, some look out for this, watch out for that. You never know about this."

Despite Officer Stalker having forgotten the 'exact wording' he used that night, scare tactics and hypotheticals certainly seemed in line with what Kelsey generally recalled being told by the officers about me, even if the young teen had confused specific language that was used with her that traumatic evening.

A young teenager cannot be blamed for not remembering the exact words said to her while she was handcuffed by the police, about ten months back, when even a professional police officer (Damien Stalker) was not able to remember the exact words he had spoken at that time! However, some terrible things were very likely said about me as part of the so-called scare tactics/hypotheticals and I believe it is appropriate for me to consider those to be defamatory.

Though memories may fade and even alter over time, Kelsey's immediate text just a few moments later that very night – at 11:41 PM on June 11, 2016 - had consisted of her claiming the cops had labeled me a 'REGISTERED SEX OFFENDER', and her demanding to know from me whether or not it was true. Though never proven one way or another, I firmly believe Kelsey's immediate text and tearful recollection to me via Facetime later that night over that of the forgetful officer, Damien Stalker, relayed in his deposition some ten months later.

Like many aspects of this complicated story, it comes down to using one's common sense to speculate intelligently about what more than likely had occurred. Also in the course of his deposition, Officer Stalker validated Kelsey's belief that they had in fact heard of me from the Deerwood hotel. The pieces of this awful puzzle were falling into place.

Though the end of the depositions brought me some relief, it would prove to be very short lived. Soon Vipperman's lawyer would begin an attack that Brian should've warned me about...

Chapter Thirteen: Vipperman's Lawyer Attacks

"The attorney we spoke with said it was feasible that if you sue someone, the defending party can ask for a forensic examination of your communication devices. If true and well known, WHY ON EARTH hadn't Brian warned me of this before I had the lawsuit?!"

They always say that the truth shall set you free. Well, perhaps. But if you're in a lawsuit and weren't warned by your attorney, the truth can literally threaten your case and cause much additional grief!

Lawsuits can turn ugly as I was quickly about to see. Unfortunately, one key aspect to Vipperman's defense of her behavior (along with her flat out denial that what the officers claimed she had stated in the police report was inaccurate), was to argue that her concerns about me were *not* defamation at all. A statement is only defamatory by law if it is untrue. Therefore, Vipperman's lawyers were determined to set out to show there may be truth to their client's concerns.

During my four and a half hour deposition, I was forced to truthfully answer any and all questions put forth to me by Vipperman's attorney... which of course I did. One question in particular he had asked, was whether or not I maintain frequent text communications with Kelsey and other youngsters in my life. Little did I realize that by answering 'yes', I was bringing more hassles my way.

When Vipperman's lawyers sent subpoenas to Kelsey and her mom for their depositions, they also asked them to hand over any and all texts they ever exchanged with me. Brian and I felt this was absolutely ridiculous. It seemed to Brian that her lawyers were on a fishing expedition to find some kind of dirt to make me look bad. And if there was no dirt to find, then they were looking to find things they could possibly twist and make me look bad to a jury. Brian suggested that I should consider objecting to this request. Brian and I discussed this matter, and then Brian decided to file an objection.

Specifically, Vipperman's lawyers seemed most interested in my text communications with Kelsey. Because I admitted during my deposition to having frequent text communications with the teenager, they were now demanding to be able to examine each one of these!

While there was certainly nothing criminal or illegal in my many communications with Kelsey or with anyone else, there were definitely things I did not wish to be made public (primarily for her protection) before a jury, a judge, Vipperman's lawyers or Gilroy! After all, there were private things that she had discussed with me in confidence (as an unofficial mentor to her) over a period of time such as:

1.) Her recollection of alleged past abusive behaviors by her father and her ongoing feelings about him.

2.) Her discussions with me about family, boys, dating, drugs, drinking and my advice to her regarding these and numerous other life issues (such as lack of motivation for school work, pros and cons of seeing a therapist, etc).

3.) Lots of discussions and gossip between her and me about mutual friends of ours who may be witnesses in this lawsuit.

Eventually there was a telephone hearing to address the complaint Brian had put in. As it turned out, when Brian finally argued the matter he said the judge had agreed to 'split the baby.' When I asked him what that meant, Brian explained it was a legal jargon that meant the judge agreed to a so-called 'compromise' to satisfy both parties. The compromise, Brian explained, was that the judge would send a letter demanding that Kelsey and her mom submit all text communications with me to the judge for *her* review. The good part for us, if there was one, was that they were not ordered to submit the texts directly to Vipperman's lawyers. Rather, the judge herself would determine if there were any relevant texts and if Vipperman's lawyers had a right to see them.

I was obviously still not satisfied with this outcome. I didn't want any of our private texts being shown to anyone at all! But I felt that at least these will be going to the judge first and she will be the one that will make the decision about whether any of them had anything to do with the case. Also, Brian assured me that there were steps that Kelsey and her mother could take to object to the ruling. But as it turned out, for some reason, the judge never did send the letter to Kelsey and her mom.

However, attacks from Vipperman's lawyer were far from over. Though I had my fingers crossed that the text message issue was behind me, it certainly wasn't. Vipperman's female lawyer brought the issue back once again. Only this time, they were not asking to retrieve messages from Kelsey and her mom. Rather now, they took the route of demanding that I submit my cell phone and entire computer to them for a forensic examination!

On Friday March 31, 2017, I received an email from my lawyer Brian. He notified me that Vipperman's lawyers were making an additional discovery request which we would now have to contend with. He went on to explain that Vipperman's lawyers had filed what was called a Motion To Compel, and were demanding I submit my cell phone and computer to a forensic examiner, thereby allowing her lawyers to review every text or email I had ever exchanged with anyone! A forensic exam, which is often used in criminal cases, would also retrieve any texts that had been deleted. I HAD NO IDEA WHATSOEVER THAT DEMANDS OF THIS NATURE COULD BE MADE IN A CIVIL LAWSUIT!!!

Although Brian said that he felt that their demand was objectionable on many grounds, he acknowledged that there was always a chance that the judge could in fact order me to turn my devices over to Vipperman's lawyers for them to sift through. Brian soon received even more demands from her lawyers asking for access to all of my medical records, the right to speak with all my previous employers dating back 20 years, and the right to speak with every organization I had ever volunteered with! As I said before, I had no idea that this could occur.

Conversely, I was also puzzled that if such far reaching demands were fair game in this kind of a lawsuit, why had Brian not imposed any similar ones on the defendant? Why did it seem as though Vipperman's lawyers were playing offense and Brian and I were stuck playing defense??

The following email from Brian on Friday, April 7, 2017 details their demands for some of this vast and unlimited information:

Sumi,

In what's becoming a daily routine, Vipperman's lawyers served some additional discovery requests today, which are attached.

The first is an additional interrogatory relating to the identities of people who heard the defamatory comments from Vipperman. What they probably don't realize is that the Court's Scheduling Order specifies that each party can ask a total of 30 interrogatories, and this one would be their 31st. Unless you have any objection, I'd like to decline to respond to this interrogatory on that basis.

The second is a request for you to sign authorizations allowing them to access documents from (apparently) most every employer and other organization with which you have ever been associated. I see this is being just another fishing expedition, and propose that we object to this request as seeking irrelevant information and decline to give them what they want.

Following this, Brian thought it would be a good idea to take my phone to a data recovery organization so they can retrieve all my texts with Kelsey. Brian suggested that we do this and then offer to share with the defendant's lawyers a whole bunch of those texts that had anything to do with

     1) My trip in November 2015
     2) My trip in March 2016
     3) The May 2016 visit that included the alcohol incident
     4) Any texts associated with the June 11, 2016 incident at Kelsey's dad's home.

Brian thought that would be a more than satisfactory offer in lieu of the 'motion to compel' hearing. Brian suggested that the judge would then feel positive about our sincere efforts and would likely deny their motion. I was willing to go along with that approach.

However, when Brian had a telephone conference with Vipperman's lawyer to try and resolve the issue, she was not willing to accept any compromise falling short of my full compliance. Unlike my lawyer who granted Vipperman two generous deadline extensions, there were no similar courtesies returned to me from the defendant's counsel. I saw this as yet another frustration and evidence that the playing field here was uneven.

As a result, a date was set to argue the motion before the judge on August 7. Arguing this additional motion, of course, meant more money from our pockets going to Brian. As of June 2017, my parents and I had spent a whopping **NINETY THOUSAND DOLLARS** on this lawsuit!!!! Brian had originally told us $60,000 through the end of a trial. Apparently he was way off. (And again of course, additional motions meant no harm done financially to the defendant, with the hotel's insurance company generously picking up her entire tab).

Rapidly losing faith in Brian, my parents and I spoke to another attorney we knew to get more perspective on forensic exams. And what I learned couldn't have made me more unhappy about the lack of information I had received originally from my lawyer. The attorney I spoke with said it was feasible that if you sue someone, the defending party can ask for a forensic examination of your communication devices. If true and well known, WHY ON EARTH hadn't Brian warned me of this *before* I filed the lawsuit?!

I would have had no problem if the judge wanted to review all my texts to determine if there were any that were relevant to the case, but I did not trust the defense legal team to keep these confidential. As we discussed earlier, a private email exchange between Gilroy and myself was mysteriously produced as an exhibit by the defense lawyers! It would therefore not be unreasonable to think that anything we shared with the defense lawyers would likely go to Gilroy and his lawyer.

If I had known about the possibility of an intrusive 'motion to compel' before I filed my lawsuit, I could have done the following:

> A. Chosen not to file the lawsuit at all – I had no issues with my information being revealed to everyone, but I did not want information about others being revealed as well.

> B. Been aggressive during discovery and could have discussed with my lawyer about seeking out forensics on Vipperman's phone and computer as it would be fair game for us to also do a review of her devices to see if she had ever mentioned anything about her "concerns" to anyone else.

In any event, we might have had a stronger case and not been faced with additional legal bills from the unexpected motion. It's hard for lay people to know these things if their lawyers do not tell them beforehand about the possibilities of motions of this nature.

But little did I know at the time that the August 7 motion would never be heard. I still had yet to endure what would be a cruel summary judgment surprise...

Chapter Fourteen: Summary Judgment Surprise

"In retrospect, this is precisely how it seems one can end up losing more and more of one's hard earned money. Had I known I was facing this second hurdle up front – and a rather expensive one - I might likely not have filed the lawsuit. And if I hadn't filed the lawsuit, my lawyer wouldn't be getting paid."

The prospect of a forensic examination on my devices was far from the only crucial thing that Brian had not informed me about before I decided to file the lawsuit.

If you take a moment to recall chapter nine of this book, you will note that at no point in 'preparing' me for this lawsuit does my lawyer Brian Niemczyk make any mention of a SECOND HURDLE I could face before trial known as Summary Judgment!

The main purpose of his letter of June 29, 2016, was to inform me of ALL possible issues and motions that could be associated with this lawsuit so I could give him my "informed" consent to proceed. Unfortunately there was no specific mention of "Summary Judgment Motion" and its associated costs and issues in that letter. Nor was there any mention of it when discussing the budget for this lawsuit. The letter did mention that the case could be dismissed due to qualified privilege associated with reporting to law enforcement, but I thought that was said in connection with the Anti-SLAPP motion that the letter talked about.

Now, several months into the case, I find out that Summary Judgment - much like the first Anti-SLAPP hurdle that Brian did mention – is yet another option available to the defendant in a defamation lawsuit. It is yet another means by which the defendant can get the lawsuit dismissed before it can reach a jury!

In asking the court to grant summary judgment, the defendant must successfully make the argument that the case presents no disputed facts for a jury to determine. This also means the defendant must argue to the judge that there is no way any reasonable juror could see the case from the Plaintiff (myself)'s point of view. The burden is higher for the defendant in asking for summary judgment, as all inferences or benefit of doubt in the arguments for summary judgment must be given to the non-moving party... meaning to me, the plaintiff.

Perhaps that is why Brian appeared so unconcerned when he alerted me in February 2017 that Vipperman's lawyers had filed a motion for summary judgment. His email to me dated February 14, 2017 at 12:54 PM, read as follows:

> "Vipperman is scheduling a summary judgment motion to be heard on May 2. I wouldn't read anything into the fact that they have scheduled a motion. It's standard practice for defense counsel to do so in lawsuits like this one. We can discuss further what a summary judgment motion is during our time together tomorrow."

In retrospect, perhaps our seemingly unconcerned attorney should have read *something* into the fact that they had scheduled this particular motion! If summary judgment was indeed such a so-called 'standard practice for defense counsel in lawsuits like this one', then why was this the first time I was hearing anything about it?? **THIS WAS OBVIOUSLY ESSENTIAL INFORMATION WHICH I SHOULD HAVE KNOWN FROM THE START... BEFORE I GAVE MY CONSENT TO MOVE FORWARD WITH THE CASE!!!!!!!!!**

During our meeting the following day, Brian expressed confidence that we should have no problem in winning the arguments for this motion - and that if by fluke we were not able to convince the lone judge up north - we could almost surely get it reversed by the MN Court of Appeals. After all, Anti-SLAPP was a much tougher hurdle and Brian had told me that we could beat that motion! Therefore, it appeared that Brian didn't feel summary judgment presented a real threat to us.

On the growing list of key things Brian didn't bother to warn me about (when he should have before the lawsuit began, back in chapter nine) was the major additional costs of filing the paperwork and making the oral argument before a judge in a summary judgment motion.

All of that combined would be about another THIRTY THOUSAND DOLLARS for me to pay Brian, plus an additional up to $6,000 to cover Vipperman's expenses should I lose the big summary judgment motion!!!! It was critical for me to have known this as Brian himself already did (as evidenced in his February 14, 2017 email) ahead of me giving my consent to move forward with the lawsuit. I was informed now only because Vipperman's lawyers had actually filed the motion!

In retrospect, this is precisely how it seems one can end up losing more and more of one's hard earned money. Had I known I was facing this second hurdle up front – and a rather expensive one - I might likely not have filed the lawsuit. If I hadn't filed the lawsuit, my lawyer wouldn't be getting paid.

And getting paid he certainly was. It was these above mentioned costs – mixed in with the whopping 18.6% increase in Brian's hourly rate beginning as of January 1, 2017 - that had brought us to the point of having spent about **ONE HUNDRED THOUSAND DOLLARS** on this lawsuit as of July 2017!!!!! The case was still nowhere close to trial.

The Summary Judgment Motion process works as follows – the moving party prepares a 30-page document asking for the case to be dismissed. The non-moving party then prepares a 30-page counter-argument which then goes back to the moving party. The moving party gets the opportunity to provide any final arguments and then the hearing takes place. Early in April 2017, Vipperman's lawyers prepared a 30-page document highlighting their arguments, which Brian had assured me was poorly written and lacking in merit.

In fact, on Thursday, April 6, 2017, I spoke on the phone with Brian. During that call, Brian strongly mentioned that the summary judgment papers filed by Vipperman's lawyers were not at all well put together. He specifically stated verbally in the call that, "We can beat all their arguments and make them look like fools for how it was written!" Certainly my long trusted attorney's counter-arguments appeared more impressive to me at the time, as did his astounding level of self-assurance. Yet again, I put my faith in my lawyer and friend of now seven years.

Regardless of how strong our counter-arguments might have been, I was still concerned about some of the arguments made by Vipperman's lawyers. In their motion asking the judge to grant summary judgment, Vipperman's attorneys had once again made a mountain out of the unfortunate but unrelated alcohol incident in May 2016. It was infuriating that they were allowed to include this irrelevant issue in their paperwork when IT HAD NOTHING TO DO WITH THE LAWSUIT!!!

To try and kill the issue for good, Brian and I obtained a sworn affidavit (written declaration) from the mother of one of Kelsey's young friends who had been involved with that situation. This was the same lady who Gilroy had repeatedly approached in his efforts to persuade others in the community to band against me.

Fortunately, this mother was courageous enough to tell the court how I had immediately informed her when I first learned what happened from Kelsey regarding the alcohol incident. She further stated that I had been far more upset over the incident than she herself had been, and that she did not blame me whatsoever for the teenagers choosing to deceive me and to make a poor decision.

The lady also acknowledged how persistent Gilroy had been in his efforts to spread defamatory information about me and to turn her against me. She even recalled how she had cautioned me to stay away from Crosby and Deerwood due to the potential safety threat imposed by Gilroy, whom she knew to allegedly be physically violent. Brian and I felt her affidavit would certainly strengthen our case.

Given all the trips I had made up north for the many depositions, I decided I would not attend the summary judgment hearing. Brian explained it would be an argument strictly between the lawyers in front of the judge, with no chance for any input from me.

Though I chose not to go, Brian stunningly reported back to me that Gilroy's attorney HAD attended! Gilroy hiring a lawyer to attend my summary judgment - much like the private emails between Gilroy and me that Vipperman's lawyers obtained – hinted at a likely alliance between Gilroy and Vipperman. In fact, Kelsey's mom had informed me back in October 2016 that Gilroy was (somehow) already aware of my lawsuit at that point in time. When I mentioned my concerns on this to Brian, he casually dismissed the notion and did not think it was necessary to investigate further.

Judges often speak a lot and have questions and comments for both sides during a summary judgment hearing. As it turned out in my case, Brian said that the judge up north had no questions or comments for either party throughout the hour-long oral argument on Tuesday, May 2, 2017. In fact, the judge's only significant question was, according to Brian, when she asked to verify how my 'unusual' last name of Mukherjee was both spelled and pronounced.***

Brian also sent me an email on May 3, 2017 at 4:05 PM, in which he stated that during the oral argument Vipperman's lawyer had "again screwed up the distinction between actual malice and common law malice, as part of the argument that your arguments about Vipperman's bad faith were just 'speculation'." I remained in awe of how Brian saw Vipperman's attorneys as so weak and inept.

Anxious as I was to learn the outcome of this matter, Brian told me that we would have to wait up to 90 long days to know the judge's decision! Should we win this big motion, the only thing standing between us and a jury trial would be a hearing on the motion to compel followed by mediation. As I learned from my earlier case back in 2011, mediation is when a financial settlement often becomes very likely.

Should we lose this big motion, my case would be in serious, serious trouble.

Aside from hassles presented by Vipperman's lawyers' motion to compel for forensics, I was able to enjoy the summer without worrying about my lawsuit. The worries reemerged however, during the final few weeks of July 2017. It was at this point that Brian asked me to collect four additional sworn affidavits from four of my friends to vouch for my excellent character. These would be used at the upcoming 'motion to compel' hearing on August 7, Brian explained, where he would argue the matter of whether Vipperman's lawyers would be allowed access to retrieve ALL text messages that I exchanged with the people up north.

Yet another difficult thing about a lawsuit that I didn't realize going in, was how dependent you can become on others to speak up in your defense. Whenever approaching someone to sign an affidavit, there is the concern that they may not wish to become involved in your legal ordeal!

Fortunately, Amanda and her father quickly signed their affidavits and sent them to my lawyer. Mark's mother, however, greatly delayed getting them signed by herself and her son Mark and returned to my lawyer, and that really stressed me. Paperwork in a lawsuit is due back on a strict schedule, and missing the deadline can mean the loss of that evidence in your case. Still, I could not get angry or impatient with Mark's mom, as I was in dire need of her assistance! Luckily, she got the affidavits into my lawyer one day ahead of the legal deadline.

As I counted down the days to the summary judgment verdict, I was plagued with dread over what it would mean to lose at this point in my case. Losing this motion would mean that the judge had in fact ended the lawsuit. Only a last chance appeal could possibly overturn such a decision. I soon found myself having nightmares over the prospect of losing my case!

Unfortunately, my nightmares became my bitter reality on the morning of Monday, July 31, 2017. Following a tearful phone call from my father, I went on the computer and reviewed this email sent to me from my lawyer Brian:

Sumi,

I have just received the attached order on Vipperman's summary judgment motion. Unfortunately, the judge decided to grant the motion. She zeroed in on the qualified privilege/good faith issue, and found that there was no genuine issue of material fact regarding Vipperman's motivations in making her report.

As you know, I believe this decision is absolutely incorrect. The judge cannot weigh evidence at this stage, and is required to grant all inferences to you in connection with this motion. In making this decision, the judge is particularly ignoring the retaliation angle because of your report to the hotel (which exists, even if there was no discipline) and is ignoring the potential implications of the 4-month delay in reporting.

In any event, this is the order the judge has handed down. Our next step, if you wish to take it, is to initiate an appeal of this decision to the State Court of Appeals. That process would have to be initiated within 60 days. I think it's best for us to sit down in person to talk about the appellate process and the procedures involved in that process. I would be happy to meet with you (and your father, if you would like) to discuss at your convenience. That meeting would be "off the clock."

You should also be aware, as I believe we have discussed at some point, that (as the "prevailing party") Vipperman now has the ability to seek to recover her "costs" in this litigation from you. This does not include her legal fees — it refers to things like her motion filing fees and some costs associated with depositions. We can discuss this issue as well.

I'm truly sorry that the order came down this way. I'm still processing how the judge could possibly view the intent issue as she did, in light of the legal standard she was dealing with. I do think you have a very good chance on appeal, if you choose to take that route.

Please contact me with any other questions.

Just like that, it was over. One year's worth of distress and financial burden, apparently, all for nothing. The judge up north had dismissed my case and now all I could do was appeal...

Chapter Fifteen: Filing An Appeal

"One important difference, I observed, was that Barbara and her co-counsel made mention of my race, color and ethnicity – effectively exploring the likelihood that it had factored into Vipperman's actions as well as those of the cops. In fact I couldn't help but wonder if even the judge up north might have been influenced by my race, color and ethnicity."

Though I was devastated beyond words at having lost summary judgment, I was relieved at least that the agonizing 90-day wait had come to an end. I was also determined to learn if my case had a valid chance on appeal. Given all the inconsistencies I had faced in dealing with Brian, I needed confirmation beyond his words that the judge up north had been wrong.

My search for an independent analysis of the judge's ruling began that very afternoon on Monday, July 31. Over the next several weeks, dad and I consulted three lawyers not associated in any way with Brian Niemczyk or his Edina, MN law firm of Hellmuth & Johnson.

After separate reviews of the judge's summary judgment order, ALL three lawyers said they felt that I had a reasonable shot at winning an appeal. It was hard to ascertain whether their determinations were based on the law or rather their interest in making money off my appeals! Because of my experience with the legal system thus far in this case, I was clearly losing trust in lawyers.

Of the three we consulted, one was a lawyer I had known well since my last wrongful termination case in 2010-2011. Her name was Barbara, and she was someone I felt I could somewhat trust. Even in how she spoke and approached my case, Barbara seemed a stronger and more effective attorney than Brian. She was older than he was, appeared more experienced and ran her own law firm in downtown Minneapolis. At this point, I was interested in the possibility of hiring Barbara to handle my appeal. Following many preliminary conversations, I finally sat down with Barbara at her office on Thursday, August 31, 2017 – one month after the summary judgment surprise.

During that meeting, Barbara explained to me that the appellate process was a tough one in itself. "The State Appeals Court is naturally reluctant to discipline the lower district court and to overturn their decisions," Barbara told me. While she was careful not to spout overconfidence as Brian typically did, Barbara said she felt I had a good argument in support of my position regarding summary judgment. "I feel after all is said and done, we have a 50/50 chance at winning on appeal," Barbara told me. Whether win or lose, Barbara informed me that the appeals process would indeed be lengthy. "It could be another 6-9 months before there is a decision in this matter," she said with a sigh.

Regardless, there did seem to be a few things going in my favor. One was that Barbara gave me a guarantee in writing that – should I hire her - my appeal would cost a flat fee of $16,000... and an additional $2,500 *only* if I prevailed. Brian told me an appeal could cost between $15,000 to $20,000. Although they were both in the similar range, by now I couldn't trust that Brian's actual numbers would be anywhere close to these initial estimates from him (based on my experience thus far with Brian's budget estimates for the case). On the other hand, I knew exactly what it would cost us if I went with Barbara. Going with Barbara therefore appeared the more economical choice for me.

Interestingly, unlike how the initial summary judgment decision was made by a lone judge up north, Barbara said the appeal would be heard by a three judge panel most likely right here in the twin cities. In order to win our appeal, we would need to convince at least two of those three city judges to overturn the lower court's decision. Barbara told me that she had argued many cases before our State Appeals Court and that she was well respected in their inner circle. She also said that defamatory accusations implying sexual misconduct were currently a hot topic within the Appeals Court.

Given this information, I decided to hire Barbara to handle my appeal instead of staying with Brian. Other than clarity on the financial aspect of the cost of appeal, I also felt that Barbara will be able to deliver a much stronger oral argument than my original lawyer. When I notified Brian of my decision, he agreed to cooperate by providing Barbara with any information she needed to help her begin the appellate process. I made sure to keep on good terms with Brian for now, as I might need him later should I win the appeal after 6-9 months!

On Wednesday, September 20, 2017, we filed our Notice of Appeal with the district court up north. In the following days, we filed the same notice with the Court of Appeals right here in the twin cities.

It excited me to know that Vipperman and her lawyers would see that I'm still in this fight. In the time that had elapsed between the decision and filing the appeal, Vipperman likely hoped that I would throw in the towel and quit. Regardless of winning or losing, I didn't feel ready to stop. I would battle Lisa Vipperman and what she had done, so long as the law allowed. Doing the right thing - over time - appeared more important than the final result.

And that final result would remain far off. Time passed quietly between the end of September 2017 and early December. As I counted down the days to the New Year, Barbara had me review her appellate paperwork which was due to be filed by December 15. Barbara met our deadline, after which Vipperman and her lawyers returned their reply on January 15, 2018. Just one week later, on January 22, Barbara filed our response to the defendant's reply.

Once again, our arguments were strikingly similar to prior ones made by Brian in his original Summary Judgment motion. One important difference, I observed, was that Barbara and her co-counsel made mention of my race, color and ethnicity – effectively exploring the likelihood that it had factored into Vipperman's actions as well as those of the cops. In fact, I couldn't help but wonder if even the judge up north might have been influenced by my race, color and ethnicity. I mentioned to Barbara that I had brought this factor up with Brian early in the case, but Brian had said to me that there was no evidence that it was racially motivated. However, what I understood from Barbara was that if someone was racially motivated in acting in a certain way, they will likely not advertise that he/she is acting that way because of the race involved.

Our second appellate brief, the one filed on January 22, seemed particularly strong and to the point. Ten pages in length, the argument consisted of the following two main points:

> 1. Vipperman's Statement Was Defamatory and Was Not Privileged
> 2. The Record is Replete with Disputed Facts on the Issue of Malice

After reviewing all ten pages, it was hard for me to imagine that the State Appeals Court would rule against us.

Still, we had yet to hear from the court as to when the appeal would be heard...

Chapter Sixteen: Appeal Is Heard

"I wouldn't change anything about yesterday, so that's good. That doesn't tell us how the Court will rule, but we gave them everything they need to make a reversal if they are so inclined. As the party who has already lost below and is asking the Court to tell that judge she screwed up, we are still coming from behind on this. So, we'll just have to wait and see- probably about 90 days."

In late February 2018, I got word from Barbara that our appeal would be heard before a three judge panel on Thursday, April 19. However, instead of occurring here in the twin cities as expected, I would have to travel to the town of St. Cloud about an hour drive away if I wished to attend. Being that I am not a morning person, and the hearing was set to begin at 10:40 AM on April 19, I planned to drive into town and rent a motel room the night before. News of a hearing date after many inactive months brought back those same anxieties over what the outcome would be.

In the days before the big hearing, I had the opportunity to speak over the phone with Barbara. Unlike during the summary judgment hearing done by Brian in May 2017 - which of course I had lost – I told Barbara that I wished to appear in the courtroom to observe the arguments and be seen by the three judge panel that would be deciding the fate of my lawsuit. Barbara said that would be fine and advised that I wear a nice suit and tie for my court appearance. She said she would try to seat me in the front row and announce my presence to the panel, even though I would not be able to speak or provide any input whatsoever.

Barbara informed me that the appeal hearing would consist of a strictly timed 35 minute oral argument between both sides' lawyers in front of the three judge panel. Barbara would get to speak for the first 15 minutes, while Vipperman's lawyer would then have the second 15 minute period to respond. And finally, Barbara would have the last five minutes to re-highlight the points of our case.

Though Barbara had her presentation well prepared, she explained that she might not be able to make all her points should the panel interrupt her with questions. Barbara said not to feel panicked if this happened, as she would have those last five minutes to tie up any loose ends.

Barbara also explained that the panel would already be familiar with the legal briefs we had filed with the court of appeals — meaning the written arguments we had submitted in support of our case in the previous months. She said the legal briefs would have considerable weight in the panel's final ruling on the matter. "Some legal experts believe once the panel reads the briefs that they have already made up their minds", Barbara told me. "Therefore, you should not panic if I am interrupted during my oral presentation."

Barbara also warned me that her comments would depend on the reactions of the panel as well as the arguments made against me by Vipperman's lawyer. "If you feel I'm not answering something as you expect I might reply, it is likely because I'm trying not to take someone's bait and fall into a trap", she explained. Barbara also told me that the panel's ruling would be influenced by how the legal issues in my case may affect other similar cases. I felt Barbara really knew how to deal with the appellate process. I felt I had made the wiser choice in selecting her for the appeal.

I felt a mixture of nervousness and excitement as I met Barbara at the courthouse on the morning of April 19. A flash of anger would soon follow, as we passed Vipperman's lawyer in the hall and observed the condescending smirk upon her face. But there wouldn't be time to dwell on my emotions. As it turned out, the panel invited us into the court to begin a full half hour earlier than scheduled!

Upon entering the courtroom, I quickly established a moment of friendly eye contact with all three members of the panel. The panel consisted of two gentlemen and one lady. I observed there were clocks in the room, like at a sporting event, to keep track of the 15 minute time periods allotted to each side to voice their oral arguments.

As my lawyer Barbara began her presentation, I was impressed with how she introduced herself and handled the panel's questions. The main question that I recall the panel asking her, was whether the statement about me being sexually abused as a child was the *only* defamatory statement that we allege Vipperman had made.

Barbara did a fantastic job of explaining how the TOTALITY OF ALL Vipperman's statements to the police carried strong defamatory implications... topped off with the striking false remark about me having a history of sexual abuse in my own childhood. Barbara did not panic or become flustered with any of the panel's questions, and came across as someone quite experienced with the appellate process.

With our fifteen minutes concluded, Vipperman's lawyer took the stage and addressed the panel. Just as she began her argument, my lawyer Brian Niemczyk strolled into the courtroom and sat down beside me! I was surprised that my primary attorney had made the long drive from the twin cities to St. Cloud to observe these oral arguments, even though I had hired Barbara for the appeal instead of staying with him.

Though I was dreading to sit through Vipperman's lawyer's presentation, I quickly noticed that the panel *appeared* to be questioning her more aggressively than when they spoke to Barbara. Through the nature of their questions, it seemed as though the panel was struggling to understand why the judge up north had chosen to grant the motion for summary judgment in favor of Lisa Vipperman. "THEY GET IT", Brian suddenly jotted down on a sheet of scratch paper he brought which he silently held up and showed me.

In doing so, Brian had his typical look of self-assurance all over his face. It was the same smug expression I felt Brian wore throughout the two years of this lawsuit; like each time he had reassured me that I had a strong and winnable case; that Vipperman's lawyers were incompetent and their motions poorly written; and that we could have beaten the Anti-SLAPP motion had her lawyers been smart enough to use it.

But for the time being it appeared Brian might *finally* be correct for once, here at last. One example of this occurred when Vipperman's lawyer began talking about the alcohol issue and her belief that multiple police agencies up north had been investigating me. "So what? What relevance does any of that have to the matters we are considering today?", a panel member pointedly asked her.

Another time was when a different member of the panel asked Vipperman's lawyer, "How can you say Vipperman's declaration to law enforcement – of all people- stating Mr. Mukherjee was sexually abused as a child was not defamatory given the circumstances?!"

And yet a third moment came when a panel member repeatedly asked Vipperman's lawyer, "How can you say there is no question about Vipperman's motivations (in reporting me to the police) when there had been a heated confrontation earlier between Vipperman and Mr. Mukherjee??"

Taken aback and evasive, Vipperman's lawyer did her best to duck these questions and instead tried to create a smokescreen of doubt. Like before, she argued that Vipperman had not been officially disciplined following my complaint about her job performance, and therefore her report to the police could not have possibly been done as retaliation against me. "What message do you wish to send to hotel employees in making this ruling?", Vipperman's lawyer implored the panel. "Do we want to send the message that it is wrong for hotel staff to report concerns they may have about children to the police?!" Fortunately, just as she tried to bring Gilroy and the alcohol back into her presentation, her fifteen minutes on the clock ran out. What a pity.

Barbara did a nice job of wrapping up our argument with the final five minutes permitted to us. She expressed, as a mother herself, that genuine concerns about the welfare of children must be taken very seriously. That being said, she also reiterated just how damaging defamatory statements are which wrongfully implicate an individual in sexual misconduct with children.

Following the hearing, Brian boldly voiced strong optimism that I would prevail in this matter. "I'm not a betting man, but if I was, I'd put my money on you to win. I like your chances," my primary lawyer stated at least twice before leaving the courthouse. Barbara, however, was optimistic, but more cautious in an email she sent to us:

"I think it went about as well as it could. There weren't any surprise questions, and I think we were able to provide good responses to the ones directed at us. I thought the other side had a harder time answering the questions and was called out a few times when she was not being responsive. We had a very active bench, meaning all three judges were asking questions, which is not always the case. The panel definitely had done their homework and understood the issues.

I wouldn't change anything about yesterday, so that's good. That doesn't tell us how the Court will rule, but we gave them everything they need to make a reversal if they are so inclined. As the party who has already lost below and is asking the Court to tell that judge she screwed up, we are still coming from behind on this. So, we'll just have to wait and see - probably about 90 days."

Much as I had waited last summer for the first Summary Judgment decision, I'd again have to wait past mid-July to learn the fate of my case...

Chapter Seventeen: Evidence Of Critical Errors and Omissions

"I had countless examples of how Brian had dropped the ball in my lawsuit. If it was malice we had needed to show to the court, then I believe that there were ways that we might have succeeded."

If there was any justice for me at all in this matter, it was the fact that I didn't have to wait until the end of July that summer to learn the court's decision. On the afternoon of Thursday, July 5, 2018, I got word from Barbara that the three judge panel had denied my appeal of the summary judgment decision.

After a grueling two year battle, I had officially lost my case. The motion that my lawyer hadn't specifically warned me about, had handed me a stunning defeat. Every effort I had made and every dollar I had spent was all a pure waste and in vain. The feeling of loss and frustration simply could not be put into words.

While Barbara said I could theoretically make a plea to the Minnesota Supreme Court, she felt my chances of winning now were about as remote as could be. Besides, appealing this any further was simply not in the cards. My parents and I were depleted and didn't have any more money to spend.

In handing down their decision, I found it revealing to note that unlike the judge up north, the MN Court of Appeals conceded that **LISA VIPPERMAN'S STATEMENTS MET THE LEGAL STANDARD FOR BEING DEFAMATORY!!!** This affirmation from the higher court felt like a moral victory after waging a war for two years. For whatever possible reason, the judge up north in her original ruling had attributed no fault to Vipperman. ****

However, the MN Court of Appeals also ruled we were not able to prove that malice existed clearly enough to overcome the qualified privilege Vipperman had – or so apparently had - in her communications with the police.

Though most anyone using common sense can see that Vipperman's conduct from day one appeared full of malice (and I still believe that a jury would likely have seen that), there was a legal standard of 'malice' we had needed to prove in court to set aside the qualified privilege and win the summary judgment motion. Once again, qualified privilege is the right everyone has to disclose concerns to the police without being punished for it. That's where we had fallen short, the higher court believed, in spite of the fact that her statements met the legal standard for being defamatory.

Given this verdict from the Court of Appeals, it appeared that without "clear evidence of malice" beyond what happened between me and Vipperman, and the email exchange between me and Dan Brown, I never had a strong enough case to have filed. And if there were possible chances to win, it appears that Brian had not

131

pursued them. I felt that a lawyer with more experience in defamation cases probably would have done a lot better than this.

Only now, almost **ONE HUNDRED AND TWENTY THOUSAND DOLLARS** later, did I sadly come to feel as though Brian Niemczyk was likely not the best fit for this defamation case. On the contrary, I had countless examples of how Brian had dropped the ball in my lawsuit. If it was malice we had needed to show to the court, then I believe that there were ways that we might have succeeded.

It is to be noted that this is not a set of generalized comments about Brian as a lawyer. In fact, as I had mentioned earlier in this book, I had good experience with Brian when he had helped me with an unemployment hearing several years back. Also, as his profile on avvo.com states, he generally focuses on employment law, commercial litigation, land-lord tenant litigation and real estate litigation. He likely has good competence and experience in these areas. It is also possible that he has had some defamation cases and some of those might have gone well. My comments here have nothing to do with any of that. My comments are simply about this specific case, what my experience has been, and my own thoughts, comments and feelings about this specific case alone. As I have said before, readers are encouraged to form their own opinions.

The following is a long list of reasons which I feel serve as evidence of critical mistakes (or errors and omissions) or of what I consider to be inappropriate. Again, these are all my observations/thoughts/feelings based on this specific case:

Brian decided to twice extend a critical deadline that helped the defendant tremendously

- The lawsuit papers containing the complaint were served to Vipperman on 08/26/16.
- Under the law, Brian said that Vipperman would have twenty days to serve a written answer to our complaint. If she declined to respond to our complaint within twenty days, Vipperman risked losing the case.
- In fact, the complaint stated, "If you do not answer within 20 days, you will lose this case. You will not get to tell your side of the story, and the Court may decide against you and award the Plaintiff everything asked for in the Complaint. If you do not want to contest the claims stated in the Complaint, you do not need to respond, A Default Judgment can then be entered against you for the relief requested in the Complaint".
- However, just 2 days before the '20 days' deadline, Brian was told that Vipperman wished to request an extension to the deadline, as she wanted to talk

with her employer – Country Inn Hotel in Deerwood - to see if their insurance company was willing to pay for her legal defense.

- Brian decided to extend the deadline as requested by the defendant. Brian and I discussed this over the phone. One of the reasons Brian wanted to allow the extension was because he thought that sometime down the road we might need some extension and then the other side will be willing to allow that if we allowed the extension here. Brian was also feeling positive about the fact that if the hotel's insurance decided to support Vipperman, then it would be easier for us to collect any judgment that we might win against her. I of course went along with Brian's guidance and suggestion on this since I did not have any experience whatsoever with bringing lawsuits.

- Since I now understand the process much better, I now believe that an error was made that allowed the defendant to get the hotel's insurance support that she badly needed to pursue her defense.

- With the large insurance company coddling Vipperman, she could afford to pay for depositions and file numerous motions against me. On her own through a private attorney, she most likely would NOT have been able to do so!!!

- If the deadline had not been extended twice, the case could have been settled right then and there. I have now heard that it is not uncommon to extend the deadline once. But instead of extending it the second time around, I believe that Brian could have tried hard to get a quick settlement (since Brian knew very well that I was extremely concerned about spending a lot of money and I was interested in getting to a quick settlement).

- Why did Brian take this approach which made this case incredibly difficult? I believe that there could be any one of the following possible reasons:
    - One possible reason could be that he could extend the case for a long time and thus earn a lot of fees.
    - He felt extension is a standard practice that he should agree with.
    - He was not looking out for his client who always wanted as quick a settlement as possible with a letter of apology and/or retraction of defamatory statements.
    - He simply did not think that this could be turned into a settlement discussion.
    - He just did not know how to turn this into a settlement discussion.
    - Maybe he was feeling fairly confident about winning the case and was feeling good about having the insurance company supporting Vipperman so we could actually collect any judgment that we might win against her.
    - Maybe there are some other reasons that I am not aware of.

- I have now heard that it is possible that Brian might have decided to allow the extensions because otherwise they would have brought a motion to get it extended and that would have cost more money. I think that extra cost would have been a problem for both sides and that could have worked as a motivation for settlement.
- Anyway, I do feel that an opportunity was lost here.

Brian should not have taken the case because this (defamation) was not one of his specialty areas

- I needed to talk with a lawyer to find out if I had a case.
- I went to Brian simply because I had known him (and trusted him) from a previous situation about 8 years back. Brian had helped me with an unemployment hearing.
- I didn't know too many lawyers in town. Since I had known Brian from this other previous situation, I decided to go to him first.
- Brian looked at what I had and told me that I had a winnable case. He did not tell me that it was slam dunk – but he did tell me that it was winnable.
- When I had met Brian in 2010, he was working for an Employment Law firm. So I knew that his expertise was likely in employment law. But I thought he would know other lawyers and would

be the best person who will be able to refer me to an appropriate attorney with focus on defamation.

- Brian wanted to take the case by himself telling me that he had done defamation cases and will be more than qualified to handle this case. I did not question him because I had known him since 2010 and had trusted him.
- However, I recently saw his profile on Avvo.com and noticed that the profile mentioned four focus areas for him and "defamation' was NOT one of them.
- I believe that he should have referred me to someone else who had more expertise in defamation cases. As I have now learned Brian really did not seem to have the experience that was needed for this case.

Brian had given us horrendously low cost estimates

- We had made it very clear to Brian that it was extremely important for us to understand what it might cost to pursue this case.
- Originally Brian gave us an estimate of $60K. This was given to us verbally.
- Later in his letter of June 29, 2016, he modified his original estimate by using the following words "depending on how the case plays out, it may reach the high five figures".
- From this we gathered (like most average persons will from this statement) that Brian was warning us that in the worst case it could go as high as 80-90K.

- However, even before the summary judgment hearing, by the end of April 2017, we had already spent close to 90K!!
- And that number did not include some of the depositions and motions that I now understand we should have undertaken to make our case winnable and establish malice (which I believe a more experienced defamation lawyer might have known).
- As of right now, we have spent about 120K – if I had won my appeal, I believe we would have spent at least another 60-80K to get through the remaining phases, including possible full length trial.
- Now that I understand the process much better, I believe that a lawyer with more experience in defamation cases might have given us the following estimates – he likely would have said that if everything goes well, we would likely be looking at 100-120K; however, if we have to deal with additional motion to compel hearings, even more depositions, summary judgment motions, etc , the total cost could go to 200K or more.
- If he had given us more realistic estimates, I WOULD NOT HAVE PURSUED THIS CASE!!!!!!

Brian always told me that it was a winnable case

- On many different occasions throughout the two year lawsuit, Brian had told me that I had a winnable case. In fact, he had told me this four months before the lawsuit even began! In an email to me on Tuesday April 5, 2016, Brian said the following on behalf of both himself and his Edina, MN law firm of Hellmuth & Johnson: "We all believe you have a good claim, and would be happy to pursue it on your behalf if you decide you would like to proceed."

- I never assumed that it was a slam dunk case – but based on his numerous comments I understood that I had better than a 50/50 chance to win the case.
- To Brian the biggest hurdle was getting beyond the possible "Anti-SLAPP" motion. He clearly explained that in his June 29, 2016, letter and in several other verbal discussions. I understood from him that once we beat the Anti-SLAPP motion, we will be home free.
- He never understood why the defendant never filed the Anti-SLAPP motion. But he was always confident that we could beat the Anti-SLAPP motion, and that it would be our biggest hurdle.
- Even at a lunch meeting with me on October 19, 2016, Brian showed surprise that the defendant hadn't filed the Anti-SLAPP motion, but during that lunch several times Brian confidently mentioned to me that we would be able to beat that motion.
- However, as I understand now, I don't believe we would have been able to beat the Anti-SLAPP motion if the defendant had brought that up. This seems to me to be another sign of inexperience on Brian's part as far as this case is concerned. I believe a lawyer with more experience in

defamation cases would likely have told us that it would be very, very difficult to beat the Anti-SLAPP motion. We couldn't even win summary judgment which was supposedly not as tough as the Anti-SLAPP motion!!!

- In his letter of June 29, 2016, he had identified several risks – I was okay with all those risks as long as there was at least a 50/50 chance to win.
- In that same letter he mentions, "I am not suggesting that you have a bad case" or "not to suggest that we could not overcome these issues and win the case", once again implying that I had a reasonable chance to win the case.
- However, I strongly believe that an experienced defamation lawyer would likely have told us what four judges have told us so far – I really did not have a case without clear evidence of malice, beyond what we already had in terms of my negative encounter with Vipperman and my subsequent email exchange with Dan Brown.

Brian did not specifically tell me about a possible "Summary Judgment Motion" before the lawsuit began

- Brian knew very well that I was absolutely new at this – I had never before filed a lawsuit.
- I had absolutely no idea what a summary judgment motion was.
- In his letter of June 29, 2016, he talks about ALL possible risks, including a lot of discussions on Anti-SLAPP, but there was no mention of summary

judgment motion and the associated issues and costs.

- Since he didn't tell me anything about it, I never knew that dealing with a summary judgment motion could by itself cost around $30,000 and if I lose summary judgment, I would have to pay an additional amount of around $6,000 for Vipperman's expenses! I wish he had included this in his letter of June 29. It would have been very useful to know about this before I made the decision to proceed with the case.
- In his letter of June 29, 2016, he had talked about Vipperman's qualified privilege and that the case could be dismissed if she was able to establish that she made a good faith report. However, I thought he had mentioned that in connection with the Anti-SLAPP motion. I had no idea that there could be yet another second motion to dismiss the case. I believe it was important for me to be aware of that before the case started.
- I only got to know about it on February 14, 2017, and only because Vipperman's attorneys had actually filed the motion. Even then Brian mentions that "I wouldn't read too much into this", indicating to me that it was not a major issue. He also indicated that "it's standard practice for defense counsel to do so in lawsuits like this one". If it was such a standard practice, then why didn't he inform me about this right at the beginning, along with the high costs and consequences of losing?

- Well, as it turned out we lost the summary judgment motion and the subsequent appeal to the higher court. Obviously, it was a MAJOR issue in this lawsuit!!!
- I believe that a lawyer with more experience in defamation cases would likely have warned me clearly about the summary judgment motion in addition to the Anti-SLAPP motion in that June 2016 letter and would have clearly told me about the risks associated with each of them.
- In his email of February 14, 2017, he mentions that "we can discuss further what a summary judgment motion is during our time together tomorrow". This confirms that he knew that he had not told me clearly about the possible summary judgment motion before the case got started.
- I believe that this was a significant omission on Brian's part in the best case scenario since I was a novice when it came to filing a lawsuit. In the worst case scenario, he might have misled me simply to pocket ALL our money; or for some other unknown reasons, he thought it was not necessary for me to know about this possibility of summary judgment motion along with the Anti-SLAPP motion before I decided to launch the case.

Brian never told me that they could file a motion to compel to surrender my phone and computer for forensic analysis

- I believe that this is yet another sign of lack of experience in cases of this nature.

- Brian had sent me a letter on Aug 18, 2016 advising us about litigation hold.
- In that letter he never mentions anything about the possibility that they could file a motion to compel me to surrender my phone and computer for a forensic analysis
- I now believe that a lawyer with significant experience in cases of this nature would probably have included this comment in his letter of June 29, 2016.
- He knew very well that I was totally new to this. I always thought that this can only happen in criminal cases, but not in civil cases. I needed to know this before I launched the case.
- I might not have filed this case if I had known that this kind of motion was possible in a civil lawsuit. I badly needed to have this information in his June 29 letter.

Brian needed to establish a clear evidence of malice

- It has become clear to me now from summary judgment order and from the subsequent affirmation by the appellate court that we badly needed to establish clear evidence of malice (beyond what we already had to start with) to overcome the qualified privilege.
- I believe that a lawyer with more experience in defamation cases would likely have known about that, and first, would have clearly warned me in his

June 29 letter that I likely didn't have enough evidence to survive summary judgment.

- And if I still pursued the case, then Brian should have done things to try and get the evidence that we needed to survive summary judgment. In his letter of June 29 he mentioned that "not to suggest that we could not overcome these issues and win the case". However, I can't see what he did to overcome these issues to survive summary judgment.
- I believe that he should have been more aggressive in his approach and should have deposed the defendant's coworker Jo Olson, supervisor Christine Yotter and the hotel owner, Dan Brown. The defendant said that the complaint written by the plaintiff did not make any difference at all – not only that she was not reprimanded but that the owner allegedly laughed right along with the defendant about the complaint! No one actually knows what happened behind the scenes regarding my complaint, and there are some situations where there were contradictory or confusing comments made by the defendant during her deposition.
- It was critical to depose the overnight coworker, the supervisor and the owner to dig deep into this in order to establish malice. Vipperman acknowledged discussing my November 2015 visit with her coworker Jo Olson, the friendly overnight employee who we were delighted to see after dealing with the likes of Vipperman that Saturday evening.
- Also, as you may recall from Vipperman's deposition testimony we had noted the following:

She claimed that she only looks at guest reservations that are arriving and leaving on the day she is working. She claimed she doesn't look ahead to see who is arriving in the near future, nor look back. She couldn't give us a reason why her supervisor Christine Yotter specifically informed her, days in advance, that I had made a new reservation to return soon.

- Right there, I believe, was a missed opportunity for Brian to have grilled Ms. Yotter over exactly WHY she felt it was necessary to inform Vipperman in advance about MY specific arrival, over all other people who were also arriving in the near future. The fact that she did so hints at the idea that Yotter and Vipperman might have had prior conversations about me and that Yotter possibly knew that Vipperman remembered and disliked me to a significant extent. This could have gone towards establishing malice, right along with interrogating Dan Brown as to what exactly he had said to Vipperman regarding my lengthy complaint about what I felt was - and had described to him as being - her terrible job performance. But for some reasons Brian, our legal expert, didn't think it necessary to depose ANY of these key individuals who Vipperman worked and associated with!!!
- I believe that Brian also should have deposed Vipperman's son, as he had been present in the room at Crosby-Ironton High School when I had given a speech there to kids about bullying in February 2016. Vipperman admitted (during her deposition) that she and her son had at least one

145

conversation about me when she was first served with the lawsuit papers in August 2016. There were likely other conversations between mother and son prior to Vipperman's call to the police in March 2016, since she already knew by that time in March that I had spoken at her son's school recently about bullying. How did she come to know of my speech??? Much as the minor child Kelsey was deposed for over an hour by Vipperman's lawyer, Brian should have been able to interrogate Vipperman's son in a search for evidence of malice towards me by Vipperman.

- Perhaps most notably, we ourselves as lay people had recommended to Brian about deposing some of these individuals and I had several back-and-forth discussions about many of these individuals! In fact, I felt certain that Brian was planning (based on his emails) to depose at least some of them to try and establish clear evidence of malice, but as it turned out, none of them were deposed. Apparently Brian thought that it would be risky to depose Dan Brown in case he ended up supporting Vipperman's views; but as per the judges, we didn't have enough to start with anyway, and therefore, it certainly would have been a risk worth taking.

▢ I also believe that Brian should have put in a motion to compel the defendant's phone and computer for forensic analysis because that would have told us if the defendant had said anything to anyone else. It is very likely that she had talked to others – such as Gilroy in particular or other co-workers - about this matter and that could have greatly helped in establishing malice.

Brian's comments about defendant's legal team

- Brian had made many comments to me undermining the capabilities of the defendant's legal team.
- He made frequent comments like: "They didn't understand the law," "If I were them I would have done this or that," "It is good that the mediator will know the law well and will be able to explain it to them," "They will look like fools for the way they have written their motion document," etc. Most of these comments were made to me verbally.
- Every time we received any motion documents from the other side, Brian always called it a "very poorly written" document and told me that they did not understand the law.
- I strongly believe that this attitude had hampered our actions in this case. One is not able to do well in situations like this if one thinks that the other side did not understand what they were doing. As it turned out, they knew EXACTLY what they were doing and they were correct!
- Brian had mentioned to me that at the summary judgment hearing he had "corrected their (meaning the defendant's lawyers) legal error on the issue of malice/intent." Since the judges ruled

147

in their favor, I tend to believe that there were probably no errors made by the defendant's lawyers on this issue.

- I don't believe that comments like these are very useful. These comments made me feel like we were dealing with inexperienced defense lawyers and we should be able to win our case for sure. However, as we all know now, that was not the case. It was an even bigger disappointment for me. So I wonder, what really was the purpose of these comments?

Miscellaneous

- Brian has always told me that he expected the case to settle much before going to trial, but it appears to me that he was simply not able to make the defendant's team feel that it would be better for them to settle.
- During the discovery period the defendant's team produced an email that was between me and Kelsey's father Gilroy. How did that email come to the defendant's team? There was clearly some sort of connection between the defendant's team and Gilroy. As far as I know, Brian never did a lot more to explore how it got there. If we had explored that link further, we might have found something that could have helped us establish malice.
- When we started the case in August 2016, Brian's hourly rate was $295. On January 1, 2017, the rate increased to $350 – an 18.6% increase! I understood that rates can change from year to

year, but that much change in one year was ridiculous. They gave us a little money back to address this issue, but it still was a key factor.

- How can a professional defamation lawyer repeatedly say that it was a good claim, but then we can't even win the summary judgment? Supposedly the Anti-SLAPP motion was a tougher hurdle than summary judgment, and Brian repeatedly told me that we could beat Anti-SLAPP. Much like his cost estimates, the reality was shockingly different from what he frequently stated. I believe that either he did not understand defamation law, or there are some other reasons that I can't think of.

- I also believe that Brian never acted like the driver or the leader in this case. I felt that he clearly let the defendant's lawyer dictate the direction of the case. It seemed to me that we were always in the defensive mode. Maybe this happens sometimes in defamation cases, but I do now believe that there were times where we could have been more aggressive in our approach.

FINAL SUMMARY

Based on my observations in this specific case, I believe that:

- There were many examples of what I perceive as errors and omissions in his handling of this defamation case.

149

- The case could have been settled very quickly if Brian had not granted two extensions to the defendant for her answers to the Complaint, and instead tried to push for a settlement.
- I most likely would not have filed this case and lost 120K if I had known any one of the following, before I gave my consent to move forward with the lawsuit. If:
  - He had given us realistic estimates, not just low ball figures.
  - He had informed me about possible summary judgment motion and all the issues associated with it.
  - He had informed me about the criticality of coming up with clear evidence of malice, beyond what we already had to start with, to survive summary judgment. This was the KEY in this case. It was now clear that we needed much more than just the lengthy email I had sent to the hotel owner to make this a winnable case or a good claim.
  - He had told me about the possibility of them filing a motion to compel the phone and computer for forensic analysis.

Regardless of how much I personally dislike Vipperman's lawyers, they were heavyweight fighters and aggressive advocates for their client. They understood defamation law correctly and left no stones unturned. They had the killer instinct needed to demolish their opponent. And last, but certainly not the least, they truly looked out for their client's best interests. Had I received the same quality representation as Lisa Vipperman did, I believe there might have been a much different outcome in this matter.

I do believe that some of these errors and omissions contributed to the undesirable conclusion of this case. These issues had really puzzled me because I had always thought of Brian to be a good and sincere lawyer. In fact, over the last 7-8 years, I had recommended Brian to many of my friends and acquaintances, whenever someone asked me about a good lawyer. Suddenly now, I was faced with these possible errors and omissions, and I started thinking of the following questions:

- Was I wrong in thinking of Brian as a good and sincere lawyer?
- Were these errors and omissions a result of inexperience or carelessness?
- Do lawyers and law firms take any responsibility at all for the negative outcome of a case that they described to the client as a "good claim"?
- Or is this how the legal profession works all over the country?

In other words, I was faced with the question of whether the whole responsibility for this loss just lies with me or does the legal profession/system have some responsibility as well? That made me think that I should look into what the appropriate processes are to find some answers.

Chapter Eighteen: Quest For Answers

"On the contrary, I was told that what I went through was probably not 'bad enough' to qualify as legal malpractice!"

If the past two years were an opportunity for me to learn painful lessons, there would be further painful lessons to follow. After the loss of my case in July 2018, we found ourselves on a quest to obtain some answers, and maybe some form of financial relief.

Having examined all of the ways that I believed my lawyer had fallen short, my thoughts went towards finding out what possible avenues we had in front of us to find some answers. We talked to several legal professionals and we gathered that we had three possible options (not in any specific order):

- File a malpractice lawsuit
- Have a meeting with the law firm's Managing Partner and express all of our complaints to him or her, elaborating on our thoughts about Brian's performance in an open and honest manner
- File a complaint to the Lawyers Professional Responsibility Board (LPRB)

We first thought of looking into filing a malpractice lawsuit but it was a hope that was very short lived. We would soon learn that the legal system is rigged to protect the lawyers and to screw over their unfortunate clients. From meeting with several malpractice attorneys in the twin cities, I realized that suing my lawyer and winning was just not something that I could accomplish.

On the contrary, I was told that what I went through was probably not 'bad enough' to qualify as legal malpractice! Numerous lawyers told us the very same thing. They explained that unless my attorney had done something wildly outrageous, such as showing up in court drunk or missing several critical legal deadlines, I did not have a good case for malpractice. Apparently, the legal system grants lawyers tremendous latitude in mishandling cases for their clients! No wonder so many of them do it.

They also explained that in order to put together a case of this nature, I would first have to hire an independent legal expert to evaluate Brian's work and determine that it was bad enough to qualify as malpractice. Depending on the complexity of the situation, that initial expert alone would cost us a whole bunch of money, maybe even up to another FORTY THOUSAND DOLLARS!!!!

Having just experienced the feeling of losing a winnable two year lawsuit, with a significant financial loss, we obviously did not have a lot of money lying around to hire a top notch expert. Anyone seeking to sue a lawyer for malpractice would likely be facing such odds. Though one malpractice attorney said he would be willing to send Brian and his firm a legally threatening letter, such a letter would easily cost us another couple of thousand dollars and would likely have no impact at all. And it seemed less likely that the letter would be effective in scaring Brian's firm into giving us any answers, let alone any possible financial relief. It was aggravating to witness how the system was rigged against average people like us!

Albeit a tough situation, a few more lawyers we spoke with suggested we consider the second approach, i.e., talking to the Managing Partner of the law firm. "Since you gave almost **ONE HUNDRED THOUSAND DOLLARS** to Hellmuth & Johnson, it is likely the managing partner of their firm would be willing to meet with you for a face to face discussion. Law firms often do that for their paying clients", these lawyers told me. "If you just go in as an unhappy client – not threatening them and not bringing a lawyer along – they might even be willing to grant you some financial relief." One lawyer even commented that, "I know for sure that if you spent that kind of money with our law firm, my managing partner would certainly be willing to take the time to listen to you and provide some answers or at least try and understand the issues".

Though the two lawyers who suggested this diplomatic approach to us turned out to be dead wrong, it did give us a rare opportunity to see a law firm's true colors. On Thursday, August 9, 2018, dad and I met with the managing partner Chad Johnson of Brian's Edina, MN law firm, Hellmuth & Johnson.

We were excited about this meeting. We felt this would give us an opportunity to talk to him about everything we had been unhappy about and were hopeful that he would give us some answers. We were also planning to ask for some financial relief, but primarily we were hoping to get answers for the various questions we had about how the case was handled by Brian.

However, from the moment he entered the meeting room with us, Chad came across to us as negative and ready to defend. It was clear to us that he was not there to "listen to understand", he was there simply to "listen to reply". We certainly did not feel that he acted like a leader who was grateful for our loyalty as one of his paying clients and was eager to listen to our complaints and concerns.

Unlike how his colleague Brian Niemczyk had tried to appease us before and during the lawsuit, Chad didn't even bother trying to charm us or extend any form of hospitality our way.

What Chad did do was sit there with a frown on his face and dismiss all of our many complaints about Brian's performance. Chad also attempted to use the fine print against me in excusing Brian's failure to tell me about the big summary judgment motion as well as the motion to compel for a forensic exam. "It states here on the initial paperwork that by filing a lawsuit, you are risking that the case could be dismissed and that private information may be exposed", he flatly stated. "Therefore, summary judgment motion and motion to compel both fall into that category. So, you *were* indeed warned of these possibilities!" Dad and I couldn't believe it. True colors were being revealed.

One can assume he was trying to protect Brian and his firm by letting us know that contractually it was all part of the deal. That is why we felt that he simply was not listening to us to understand our issues. However, we were not there for a contractual debate, we were there to let him know that we did not feel we received the value we expected to receive from his law firm after paying $295-$350 an hour for one of his lawyers and were hoping to receive some reasonable responses.

As a contrast, we felt very strongly that we received great value for the money we paid to Barbara for her work on the appeal, even though I lost my appeal. I felt Barbara was on top of things at all times, she was always thinking of new ways to present the situation, she was being very respectful about the abilities of the defense lawyers, she was very good in preparing the documents and she was well prepared for the hearing and did very well in front of the judges. On the financial side, we knew exactly what we were going to pay her and there were no issues at all. I felt I got the value I expected from her. But in case of my interactions with Brian, I certainly did not feel that I received the value that I deserved.

Chad also had the gall to sit there and share with us his belief that all four judges (the judge up north and the three appeals court judges in St. Cloud) had been wrong in their decisions to grant summary judgment in Lisa Vipperman's favor. "They concluded they knew what was in Lisa Vipperman's mind and what she had been thinking when she approached the police. That should have been a question for a jury to decide and the case should have been remanded for trial. Not Brian's fault that they ALL ruled incorrectly!", the senior partner brazenly asserted.

I find this very interesting. This is like a football game when a referee makes a call – the coach does not like the call and challenges the call (which is like an appeal) – the referee then reviews the replay in association with other senior officials and comes back to confirm the call – but the coach and the players continue to blame the officials for losing the game for them!

They really need to move on from blaming the officials and start looking at themselves to take some responsibility for the loss and figure out what they did wrong and what they could have done better to win the game. It was clear that neither Chad nor Brian was going to take ANY responsibility for the loss. Brian was not only a part of my team, he was the leader, but yet, he was not going to take any responsibility for losing my case.

Overall, this was an extremely disappointing meeting. We thought, as a managing partner of a law firm, Chad will take some responsibility for not being able to help me in this lawsuit. We were not expecting that he would say that "we screwed up badly". But we were expecting that he would say something like, "I am really sorry that we were not successful in this lawsuit. We really felt that we had a reasonable shot, but in the legal world, pieces don't always fall the right way. Maybe there are some things that could have been done differently, but I can assure you that Brian did his best in trying to win this for you. Sometimes there are judgment calls involved and it's not always easy to predict how the calls will work out".

Some comments like that would have given us the feeling that at least they were taking a measure of responsibility. Instead what we got was an extremely strong defensive stand and that was disheartening.

For me, there were many unanswered issues/questions that I felt Chad or Brian should have addressed. Here is a simplified list:

- **Why** didn't I get a more realistic estimate? We are aware that estimates cannot be expected to be exact, but knowing very well that we were concerned about the financial impact, why didn't Brian try to give us a better estimate BEFORE I consented to move forward?
- In his June 29, 2016 letter Brian did warn me about the Anti-SLAPP motion and that the case could be dismissed, but **why** did that letter not mention anything specifically about the possible summary judgment motion?
- **Why** was I not told that a summary judgment motion could cost us another $30K?
- **Why** was I not informed about the possibility of a motion asking for a forensic analysis of my phone and computer? Yes, I was told that things could come out that might hurt my reputation further

and I was aware of that, but that is not the same thing as a forensic analysis of my electronic devices!

- **Why** didn't we ask for a forensic analysis of Vipperman's phone and computer – that could have given us some possible evidence of malice?
- **Why** didn't we do more depositions to try and establish clear evidence of malice, as discussed in detail in Chapter 17?

Chad and/or Brian could have addressed all these issues/questions for us. Brian knew that we were having this meeting with Chad. We had handed a document to Chad describing all our comments and issues. I feel very certain that Brian had seen that list after our meeting with Chad. Then why didn't Brian give me a call and say, "Hey Sumi, I understand you have some questions/concerns about my decisions and actions. How about coming over for a face-to-face meeting so I can address these questions/concerns with you?" Also, Chad could have brought Brian in to the meeting with us to address these concerns right then and there. Chad could have also asked us to come back another day so we could meet with both Brian and Chad to get their responses to these outstanding questions/issues. But none of that happened.

I believe it would have been a classy move to get Brian to attend a meeting with us and address these concerns. It would have been an even classier move to pay us back a bit of money (say $10K) as a goodwill gesture. Although we had asked Chad to consider sharing the financial burden equally with us because of the unanswered issues we brought up, we never expected that they would agree to do that. But we did think that they would be willing to pay us some money back. I strongly feel that with the rate we were paying, refunding something like $10K back to us would not have hurt them at all financially.

These gestures would have certainly told us that the firm was taking some responsibility. Without any of that, we were left to feel that the firm was clearly not taking ANY responsibility for the loss. Instead, they were just happy to say that the four judges made the mistake!

After our experience with Brian and Chad, I have come to understand why many people use various 'negative expressions' when they talk about lawyers. I never felt that they ever showed any concerns whatsoever about the impact this case had on us and how we felt about the whole thing.

Before our hour long meeting ended, Chad let it be known to us that he was aware that I would not have a strong malpractice case against Brian should I consider going that route. Upon final parting, Chad said he would speak to the law firm's other top partners to see whether or not to grant us any financial relief.

Apparently, it was not a difficult decision for the group of lawyers to make. The very next day, on Friday, August 10, 2018, Chad sent us an email denying us any form of relief, whatsoever. In that email he of course reconfirmed that he disagreed with our assessment of Brian's performance in this matter. Here are some of the comments he made in that email and what our thoughts were on those comments:

He mentioned that I was advised of the litigation risks before commencing the litigation

- Well, we never said that I was not advised of the litigation risks. My issue was that I felt that some of the key risks were left out of the letter Brian had sent me to advise me of the litigation risks. I felt it was critical for me to have known those risks as well, considering that Brian was aware that this was my first lawsuit.

Chad mentioned that his law firm's representation and the fees charged for that representation was consistent with the Master Hourly Retainer Agreement

- Well, we never said that the fees charged were inconsistent with the Retainer Agreement. Our issue was more with the budget estimate.

He mentioned that I was notified that given the adversarial nature of the legal system, they cannot and do not make any guarantee of success in the ultimate outcome of these matters, or regarding the time which will have to be spent on a proceeding.

- Well, I never asked for or expected a "guarantee' of positive outcome in this matter. I also did not expect a "guarantee" regarding the time which will have to be spent on the proceeding. All I expected was a better estimate which I believe could have been possible.

Chad also mentioned that "you complained that Brian's initial estimates of legal fees proved incorrect"

- Well, we never used the word "incorrect" to describe Brian's estimate, because any estimate can be correct depending on the assumptions made to arrive at the estimate.

He also mentioned that "estimates were given at the beginning of representation, before key facts and strategies were raised in the litigation".

- Well, I disagree. I believe that all key facts were known fairly well when the estimates were given. It is true that it was not known what motions would be brought forward by the defense – but Brian was aware of the possible Anti-SLAPP motion, and based on his experience with other cases he should have thought of other possible motions by the defense (e.g., he told me later that Summary Judgment is a very standard motion typically brought forward by the defense). Since he was aware of this possibility, he could have included appropriate cost estimates for this and other possible motions and prepared a far more realistic cost estimate. In his email of April 5, 2016, Brian mentioned that "I would be happy to prepare a proposed litigation budget for you, which would outline the estimated costs of each phase of the case." I believe that if he really had done that carefully, then he would have thought of the various possible motions for each phase of the case.

Chad then mentioned that his firm provided us with detailed monthly invoices of legal fees and costs, and that we had paid the same without issues. He further mentioned that if we had concerns regarding the costs of litigation during the process, then I had the sole authority to stop that representation.

- Again, it seems like we were just not seeing eye-to-eye on this. Of course we paid all the bills on a very regular basis, as he said. However, I don't believe that stopping the representation was really a reasonable option. It didn't make any sense to me. For example, by the end of the discovery phase we had already spent close to $60K. Did it make sense for me to stop the representation at that point knowing that there are two outstanding motions (summary judgment and motion to compel) still out there to be addressed? If I had gone to someone else at that point, it would only make sense that our costs would have been even higher because the new attorney would need time to get up to speed with everything that had happened until then.

Once again, the point was not about the costs accumulating during the proceeding – the point was about a more realistic cost estimate before we got started.

I still think that it would have been a nice move by them if Chad would have decided to have another meeting with us and had included Brian in that meeting so he could explain what his thoughts were on these issues. It is possible that they did not want to do that because Brian likely did not have satisfactory answers in response to all our concerns. It is possible that by trying to answer our questions Brian could have dug a deeper hole for himself, and maybe that's what they were concerned about.

I believe that all our concerns brought out legitimate issues and deserved satisfactory responses. However, the most concerning and puzzling one is about not doing enough to establish evidence of malice. As the appellate judges mentioned very clearly, it was essential to come up with clear evidence of malice to overcome the qualified privilege. I had several discussions (and email exchanges) with Brian about deposing 3-4 more people to try and see if we could get evidence of malice.

Even non-lawyers like us felt concerned that it was likely that more evidence was needed to show malice on

Vipperman's part. Brian not only agreed, he even talked about (in an email) the things he would ask them during the depositions. But somehow he never followed through on any of those depositions. I now strongly believe that this had a significant impact on the outcome of this case.

Interesting to note, that Chad's email did not address the issue about why some of these depositions were not taken. Regardless, it was time to move on.

Chapter Nineteen: Lawyers Professional Responsibility Board

"So much for 'professional responsibility', as far as I am concerned. The only silver lining in this at all, is for you as the reader of this book. You can benefit from my awful experience and clearly know ahead of time what you can expect from lawyers and the legal system here in Minnesota, and also likely anywhere else around the country."

With our hopes of getting answers and/or some financial relief reduced to rubble, we shifted our focus to the one area where we might still have a shred of influence: Taking questions and concerns to an organization responsible for evaluating a lawyer's performance.

In our many conversations with attorneys following the loss of our case, we were told we could make a lengthy complaint about Brian to the Lawyers Professional Responsibility Board for the state of Minnesota.

According to several attorneys and the board itself, there would be three possible steps in processing our complaint. The first step would be for us to submit the complaint and for the board to determine if there was sufficient evidence to investigate the matter any further.

The second step, if achieved, would be for the board to conduct a thorough and intense investigation of Brian's conduct. And third, following their investigation, the board would make a determination as to whether or not they would mete out discipline to my lawyer. One of the malpractice attorneys we consulted said he could assist us in organizing our arguments before we submit a final draft to the board for their possible consideration.

Upon completing an online search, we found the website for the board to be the following: lprb.mncourts.gov. On further investigation, we came across a legal reference document on the website called *Minnesota Rules Of Professional Conduct*. The document, about 120 pages in length, provides clear and concise guidelines of exactly what criteria must be met in order to argue to the board that a lawyer violated Minnesota's rules of professional conduct. It's one thing to believe your lawyer has done you wrong, but it is quite another thing to compile ALL the evidence necessary to support your critical points!

After thoroughly reading the entire document and working on our arguments for months, we came up with a draft showing why I believed Brian violated Minnesota's rules of professional conduct in his duties as a lawyer.

After paying an attorney $500 to look it over and make additional changes, the following is an overview of the final revised copy of our arguments which we submitted to the Lawyers Professional Responsibility Board in November 2018. I am providing a brief overview here because you as the reader are already aware of all the details that I have described earlier. Also, the summary below doesn't include the numerous email and document attachments which we sent along with this paperwork:

OVERVIEW OF OUR COMPLAINT

We had carefully reviewed the document "MN Rules of Professional Conduct" that we had downloaded from the LPRB website. Based on what we had learned from that document, we strongly believed that Mr. Niemczyk's actions or lack of actions in the following four general areas were unethical:

- **Misleading cost estimates**
- **Lack of adequate information for informed consent**
- **Competence issues**
- **Behavior issues**

We cited the following comments from the "MN Rules of Professional Conduct" document to support our complaint:

- Lawyers must provide a client with an informed understanding of the client's legal rights and obligations and explain their practical implications.
- The lawyer must make reasonable efforts to ensure that the client or other person possesses information reasonably adequate to make an informed decision. Ordinarily, this will require communication that includes a disclosure of the facts and circumstances giving rise to the situation,

any explanation reasonably necessary to inform the client or other person of the material advantages and disadvantages of the proposed course of conduct and a discussion of the client's or other person's options and alternatives.

- A lawyer need not inform a client or other person of facts or implications already known to the client or other person; nevertheless, a lawyer who does not personally inform the client or other person assumes the risk that the client or other person is inadequately informed and the consent is invalid.
- In determining whether the information and explanation provided are reasonably adequate, relevant factors include whether the client or other person is experienced in legal matters generally and in making decisions of the type involved.
- A lawyer shall explain a matter to the extent reasonably necessary to permit the client to make informed decisions regarding the representation.
- The client should have sufficient information to participate intelligently in decisions concerning the objectives of the representation and the means by which they are to be pursued.
- Informed consent requires that each affected client be aware of the relevant circumstances and of the material and reasonably foreseeable ways that the conflict could have adverse effects on the interests of that client.
- A lawyer shall provide competent representation to a client. Competent representation requires the legal knowledge, skill, thoroughness, and

preparation reasonably necessary for the representation.

- Clients normally defer to the special knowledge and skill of their lawyer with respect to the means to be used to accomplish their objectives, particularly with respect to technical, legal, and tactical matters.
- A lawyer should demonstrate respect for the legal system and for those who serve it, including judges, other lawyers.
- A lawyer should maintain a professional, courteous, and civil attitude toward all persons involved in the legal system.

Though I had lost the summary judgment appeal back on July 5, we didn't get this long thought out report completed and in the mail until November 9, 2018.

In early December 2018, we heard back from the LPRB. It was a disappointing response. They informed us that "the Director has determined not to investigate our complaint". This would mean that I still would not get the answers I was looking for in terms of the things that Brian did or did not do that I felt had significant negative impacts. Their letter did also mention that "if you are not satisfied with the Director's determination, an appeal may be made within 14 days". I thought about that, and at first, I was not sure it would be any good to spend any more time on this to send an appeal.

However, after studying the details their letter included about how they evaluated our complaints, I realized that they did not seem to completely understand what we were trying to say in our original letter and in some cases they felt the situation was not serious enough to warrant an investigation. The following is a brief summary of their comments along with my thoughts about their response:

- Regarding the first complaint about budget estimates they mentioned that "it is not necessarily a violation of the ethics rules for a lawyer to have been incorrect in estimating the true cost of litigation". They also mentioned that "you were billed hourly and received monthly billing statements, so you were on notice of the mounting legal fees". Reading these comments it seemed to me that we needed to clarify that we were not complaining about "incorrect" estimates – we were complaining about not providing "realistic" estimates under the specific circumstances. I also felt it would be necessary to clarify that we were not complaining about how we were being billed.

- Regarding our second complaint about lack of adequate information for informed consent, they termed it more as "poor communication". They felt that Brian was communicating with me about Summary Judgment; but they failed to see that our complaint was not about Brian not communicating with me about this – our complaint was about not informing me about the possibility of this motion "before" I gave consent to move forward, not several months later into the case. So I felt we needed to clarify this as well.

- Regarding our third complaint about competence issues, they felt that our complaints were not about any competence issues, but were allegations of negligence, poor quality representation or malpractice. Again I felt we needed to clarify that our complaints were not just about negligence.
- Regarding our fourth complaint about unprofessional comments and behavior, they felt that such conduct would fall short of the profession's best standards, but would ordinarily not violate a Rule of Professional Conduct. On this point I felt there was no need to clarify any further. We cannot do much more if they do not want to investigate possible conduct that could potentially fall short of the profession's best standards (in their own words).

Therefore, we decided to put together an appeal with further clarifications on the three issues I discussed above and mailed it back to them on Dec 12, 2018. They might still not want to investigate this any further, but I thought it was important that I tried to make sure that the Board had a clearer understanding of my issues.

Around the end of February 2019, we received a letter from the Board informing us that the appeal was reviewed and it was determined that no investigation will be done on this matter. It was noteworthy that this letter from the Board was a very short one – only 3 or 4 sentences long.

The Board Member, who evaluated our appeal, was Virginia Klevorn. Virginia was a member of the Minnesota House of Representatives, representing District 44A. She basically stated that there was no clear and convincing evidence of a violation of the Minnesota Rules of Professional Conduct and therefore they were closing the Board's file on this case. It was interesting that they did not want to get into any kinds of details about why they thought my complaints and further clarifications did not provide the necessary evidence for the Board to initiate an investigation.

For example, it would have been useful to know why the information we provided supporting our views of Brian's performance on this case is not regarded as "clear and convincing evidence" by the Board, or why the details we provided about the information (such as summary judgment issues) that I needed to know before giving my consent to move forward with the case is not considered to be important enough by the Board to have violated the MN Rules of Professional conduct. I believe that it was reasonable for me to expect some explanation, but their short letter did not include any of that.

After some thought, we decided to send a polite letter back to Virginia Klevorn and the Board requesting a meeting to discuss this matter simply for us to understand why these issues did not rise to the level needed for investigation. Here is the letter we sent in early March, 2019:

Dear Ms. Klevorn,

We received your letter dated Feb 22, 2019, informing us that your review of this matter did not find any clear and convincing evidence of a violation of the Minnesota Rules of Professional Conduct, and that the case was now closed. We are of course disappointed about this verdict, but we understand that this is where it now stands.

However, we are still left with a number of questions that remain unanswered. We would therefore appreciate it very much if you would kindly give us some time so we can meet with you to get some clarity on the various issues that we had described in our original complaint and in our subsequent appeal. It may just have to do with interpretation of the Minnesota Rules of Professional Conduct, but it would be extremely beneficial for us to get a better understanding of why the issues we described did not rise to the level of being worthy of an investigation.

Please understand that we are not trying to put in another appeal, or to argue about the findings, or to demand an investigation, etc – we are simply trying to understand the details about how our complaint was viewed by the Board and why it did not meet the threshold needed for an investigation. We believe that one meeting will likely clarify all our questions.

We hope that you would kindly consider our request favorably and will be willing to have a meeting with us for these clarifications.

We look forward to hearing back from you soon.

I know that the letter was received by the Board on March 8, 2019. I am still waiting for a response back from them!!

So much for "professional responsibility", as far as I'm concerned. The only silver lining in this at all, is for you as the reader of this book. You can benefit from my awful experience and clearly know ahead of time what you can expect from lawyers and the legal system here in Minnesota, and also likely anywhere else around the country.

Based on my experience I believe that the board's 'professional responsibility' is a courtesy extended to the lawyers... and certainly NOT to any of us who may become their unfortunate clients!

Chapter Twenty: The Elephant In The Room

In early June 2020, basketball superstar Kareem Abdul-Jabbar made the following eloquent statement on racism: "Racism in America is like dust in the air. It seems invisible – even if you're choking on it – until you let the sun in."

Although it is all too often staring us in the face, we never like to focus on the issue of race and its possible role in such negative situations as the one in my true story. As mentioned in Chapter One, my status as a dark skinned ethnic minority has haunted me throughout the course of my life. With the epidemic of racism still rampant across America as of 2020, I know that stories like mine are far too commonplace.

Though I have no concrete proof to say that my race/color was a factor in Lisa Vipperman's mind, I certainly harbor my personal opinion that it played a role in her vindictive behavior. It doesn't stretch the imagination to presume that Vipperman might have felt especially irked that a man of color had the gall to demand respect from her at the pool (in front of cheering teenagers) and then later to criticize her job performance in great detail to her employer. Clearly, her apparent dislike for me upon our very first interactions supports the idea that my race/color was a factor. I had been warned of the alleged prevalence of racism up north by Amanda's grandmother who was dealing with cancer.

One possible example of this alleged racism in that area may include the fact that to my knowledge - as of January 2020 and in prior years - at least two of the schools in the Crosby/Deerwood MN area did not observe the federal holiday that is Martin Luther King Jr. Day. According to an online search, on November 3, 1983 President Ronald Regan signed a bill marking the third Monday of January, as Martin Luther King Jr. Day, to honor the slain black civil rights leader. In January 1986, the first national Martin Luther King Jr. holiday was observed.

Yet 34 years later in January 2020, and to my knowledge also in previous years, both the Crosby-Ironton High School and the Cuyuna Range Elementary School (in Crosby) still held school for students on this national holiday during which the U.S. Postal Service, banks and most other schools nationwide were closed! I personally find this fact to be rather peculiar and disturbing, as these same two schools do indeed observe other national holidays such as Presidents' Day in February. Although one might argue that this doesn't directly confirm racism, there are other examples that certainly do.

One example of this alleged prevalence of racism up north was disclosed to me directly by my ex-girlfriend's daughter, Amanda. In fact years after getting to know Amanda – my ex-'s daughter who lives up north in Crosby – the teen revealed that she had strongly disliked me when I first began dating her mother. She and I even chuckled together as we recalled how poorly Amanda had treated me when her mother and I met in the fall of 2013, and in the months that followed.

Along with her deep attachment to the man who had dated her mother right before me, Amanda then admitted she had also detested me in part because of my brown skin color! I was honestly flabbergasted upon hearing this from Amanda, and so many years after the fact. I never had the slightest inkling in all that time that my race/color had mattered at all to her!!! Amanda further disclosed that her Crosby, MN classmates felt the same way as she initially had, with one friend asking her bluntly upon first seeing me, "WHAT THE HECK IS YOUR MOMMA DOING WITH THAT INDIAN GUY?!" Had it not been for a trust built up from years of friendship and mentoring, Amanda never would have disclosed to me the prejudice she had once felt.

Honest disclosures to me like Amanda's revealing racism were not uncommon during my years at school growing up and remained so in the decades to follow. Many of these people, such as Amanda, often revealed it to me after having gotten to know me personally and eventually liking me as an individual. Assuming white babies are not automatically born with racist feelings towards people of color, one has to conclude it is very much a learned response or behavior.

If so, WHERE and HOW did the numerous white people who expressed these sentiments to me come to learn and accept such beliefs as being standard and normal? When and where had Amanda and her classmates heard and understood that it is OK to dislike an individual immediately if they are of Indian descent or any person of color??

Being such an individual, I've come to feel as though I am often deemed 'guilty until proven innocent.' In other words, I am initially viewed in a very negative light and have to go out of my way to first PROVE that I am a good person and thereby worthy of humane treatment and respect.... just as if I was white!! In this sense you are often at a big given disadvantage. I'm guessing other people of color are also quite familiar with this predicament. One can wonder if this was a factor in play when I first encountered Lisa Vipperman at the Deerwood hotel.

I also heard from reliable sources up north that a certain individual associated with the case had allegedly referred to me with the racist, derogatory term of "SAND NIGGER", right along with allegedly voicing their desire to "CUT SUMI'S THROAT." On the less violent side of racism, one of the teens from that area told me several times that her father and other family members had long prohibited her from ever dating ANY individual of color. "If you date or marry someone of a different race/color, don't expect us to be at your wedding!" was apparently what her dad and other family members had said to her.

"White belongs with white and black belongs with black and so forth", the teen recalled hearing on numerous occasions throughout her lifetime. Her disclosures made me wonder if familial pressure regarding race was to blame for some very positive courtships I'd had in the past that had suddenly ended for no apparent reason.

Still another friend from up north had told me that a relative of hers felt convinced I was a bad person. When I asked her why, my friend replied, "Well, my relative feels that I shouldn't be friends with a person of a different race." I guess that just about says it all. Years later, following a very nice visit with my friends in the Deerwood area in late summer 2020, I was informed that a close relative of the group I visited, apparently disliked me so much that my friends were afraid to even mention my name around this individual! This was a shock for me to hear, since I had several seemingly friendly interactions with that same relative in question during my summer visit. My friends were surprised also, as they made the eloquent statement "the relative doesn't even hardly know Sumi at all, so how can they dislike him so much?!"

I feel my story should serve as a warning to ALL ethnic minorities living throughout the United States; that we may find ourselves more likely to become targets in some environments. Of course, it would be different if we were not who we are, i.e., if we were white. Though this can and does happen anywhere in America, smaller rural towns - it certainly appears - may present an increased risk for us.

According to information available online, as of 2017, Crosby had a population of 2,344 while Deerwood's population was just 521. Vipperman's home town of Ironton, MN, had a population of just 561 residents.

In sharp contrast, where I live, a two hour drive away in the city of Plymouth, the population in 2017 was 78,395 residents. And the much bigger nearby city of Minneapolis had a staggering population of 422,331 people in 2017! Naturally, individuals in larger cities with far greater populations are much more likely to come into contact with dark skinned ethnic minorities like myself. The lack of exposure to persons of color in much smaller cities may be a factor which influences ignorance and racism in those places.

Regardless, there is no excuse for it and it cannot be tolerated! **WE ARE ALL HUMANS REGARDLESS OF OUR RACE, COLOR AND ETHNICITY!!!!!!** It boggles my brain as to how and why racism still has a place in our world. But it clearly does.

In my comments about smaller towns, I'm certainly NOT attempting to say that such places aren't filled with kind and wonderful people who could care less about what race or color a person is... including many of my closest friends and those who stood up for me in this lawsuit! We minorities just need to watch our backs for the ones who feel we don't belong.

Though it may qualify as speculation, I do not feel I would have been treated nearly as poorly by Lisa Vipperman had I been white, as she was. One merely needs to look at her dislike upon first glimpse of me, her unprovoked rudeness, her questioning of the kids (instead of asking me as the paying adult guest), her behavior at the pool and then her false report months later to the Deerwood police. I felt treated as a second class citizen by her, right from the start and throughout. Common sense leads me to believe that she does not treat most other guests in these ways!

I also believe, albeit speculation, that some of the small town police were quicker to judge me poorly because of my race and color. Even the judge up north herself – who unlike the MN Court of Appeals judges attributed no fault at all to Vipperman – might have been influenced by my race, color and ethnicity.

The fate of being treated as different doesn't appear to change over time. It seems to remain a heavy burden which we minority people must carry – in both big ways and small ways – day in and day out. Though I did not prevail in court, I am grateful that I was able to show Vipperman that there are folks who will stand up and fight for their rights honestly and ethically! Hopefully she never again will commit such a similar kind of act.

The point of this lawsuit was to teach someone a lesson. Let us hope that the lesson was learned. I hope that my story will motivate others to fight for their rights as well.

Along with the blame on my defamer Lisa Vipperman, I am also tremendously ashamed of the person(s) in charge of running the Country Inn Hotel in Deerwood, Minnesota at the time of this lawsuit. And they too ought to be tremendously ashamed of themselves!!!

The following is a news article from July 2018, describing a strikingly familiar scenario where a white Subway employee wrongfully called the cops on an innocent black family in Georgia. As you read it, you will see the uncanny similarities this true story has to my true story. The huge difference, however, is how the Subway organization stepped up and addressed their employee's egregious misconduct:

After calling 911 on black family, Subway worker placed on leave

Hope Schreiber,Yahoo Lifestyle Mon, Jul 9 2018 9:44 PM CDT

A Subway employee called the police on the Dobson family, claiming they were behaving suspiciously. (Photo: Felicia Chambers Dobson via Facebook)
The <u>Subway employee</u> who called the police on a black family eating dinner has been placed on administrative leave.

The white female employee of the Subway store in Newnan, Ga., called 911 because she believed the family visited the restroom a "suspicious" number of times. On the call, she said she thought the family planned to rob the restaurant.

You know, a family robbing — bring the kids along!

The Dobsons were on their way home from their grandmother's birthday party when Othniel and Felicia Dobson, along with their children, aged 19, 13, 12, and 8, stopped to have dinner.

"One employee, a white woman named Sandra, wasn't that friendly — it seemed like she was making our sandwiches begrudgingly — but we didn't pay much attention," Felicia, 40, told Yahoo Lifestyle. "We paid for our food, sat at a table, and I read a few pages of my book."

For the drive, the family had packed their car full of snacks, including juice, which they drank from cups they had purchased for ice.

Sandra also allegedly told police the family filled their water cups with soda.

WFMY-TV reports that the worker is now on administrative leave. The franchise owner and the police officer who responded to the call have both apologized to the family.

A spokeswoman for Subway said in a statement: "Respect for every individual is a core value of Subway. It is our expectation and each Franchisee's goal to make sure that every guest will always be treated with the respect and integrity they deserve. The Franchisee has personally apologized to the family and the employee in question has been placed on leave until a full review is completed."

Rosh Patel, the franchise owner, released the following statement: "I take this very seriously and I am fully investigating. I have interviewed all employees involved and will reach out to the family to offer my sincerest apology. I have also used this opportunity to reiterate to my staff the importance of making everyone feel welcome and providing great customer service."

Tragically, incidents like this one and mine against dark skinned ethnic minorities are far from uncommon. Also in July 2018, a CVS Health Store in Chicago apologized to a black woman after a white manager wrongly accused her of using a counterfeit coupon and called the police on her! Most recently in May 2020, a white woman in New York called the police on a black man who was bird watching, after the gentleman asked her to leash her dog in Central Park. In retaliation, she called 911 twice and falsely claimed that the black man had threatened her and then also tried to assault her. In this most recent case, the woman faced a misdemeanor charge of falsely reporting an incident. These are just a few of many such cases we are publicly hearing about now, hence the reason why people of color appear to be at a higher risk for such mistreatment throughout the U.S.

Even in a world where these things do happen, dignified professionals can make a big difference to combat it. The operators of the Country Inn Hotel in Deerwood, Minnesota need to be schooled by Rosh Patel and CVS Health Store about professionalism and customer service! As awful as those true stories were, I feel mine is an even worse example of premeditated misconduct.

Along with probable racial undertones, Vipperman's actions, I firmly believe, were done as revenge for a prior altercation and subsequent complaint to her employer. And in doing so, she sought to have me labeled a sexual predator and, in addition, ruin future speaking opportunities in that region. She put both my professional reputation and personal safety in serious jeopardy! There is no false label as hideous and awful as that of a child molester!!!!!

Detestable as the actions were of the Subway worker and CVS Manager, they at least called the cops RIGHT AWAY and not nearly half a year later (like Vipperman did)!! They could potentially argue they had acted *immediately* on their alleged 'concerns', wrongful and likely racist as those concerns were.

Lisa Vipperman cannot even make that argument, and to think that the Country Inn Deerwood chose to defend her in the lawsuit disgusts me to this day. After all, I had been a repeat customer and would have continued to bring my business to them for many years had this never occurred.

Again, one cannot ignore the possibility that my status as a dark skinned minority might have factored into the organization's decision to support their employee's wrongdoing. According to Vipperman's deposition testimony, the Country Inn Owner Dan Brown (who was the owner in November 2015) had actually laughed along with Vipperman about my lengthy complaint! "I believe we chuckled because we thought the complaint was ridiculous," Vipperman had testified under oath.

If indeed true as she stated, what was so ridiculous about my expectation that Vipperman exhibit far better customer service skills as ALL of the other staff there already did? My complaint was specific, type written and explained in great detail. I was a repeat and paying adult customer of their established business. To this day I fail to see what exactly qualified it as a laughing matter. Was it viewed as 'ridiculous' by Vipperman (and also by Dan Brown according to Vipperman) because a human being of my race and color has little credibility to them??

Aside from the now presumably fake apology I received via email from Dan Brown, the organization never apologized to me for Vipperman's defamatory call to police; apparently never disciplined Vipperman for misconduct in November 2015 or in March 2016 and rewarded her atrocious behavior by funding her entire defense! I had sued Lisa Vipperman and NOT the hotel. The hotel did not have to back her up. Yet they did. And in doing so they gave me the message that I have zero value as a customer to them, or even as a human being, for that matter!

Good management is the heart and soul of a successful operation. What kind of business were these folks running at Country Inn Deerwood where the owner allegedly 'chuckles' at a genuine customer complaint and supports an employee who reports to the police about their guest with made up, unsubstantiated defamatory statements?!

Vipperman's twisted choices cost her organization my continued business as well as the possible inevitable rise in premium rates for the hotel's insurance carrier because of the tens of thousands of dollars in legal fees paid to the insurance company's lawyers. Regardless, the organization felt it was a worthwhile cause to not reprimand her, to continue her employment and to fully defend her against me, their paying guest and a person of color.

This ordeal ranks up there with the worst customer service experiences of all time. One can only ponder the reasons why I was treated so poorly in this situation. ***

Chapter Twenty One: How Not To Get Screwed Like I Did

"My advice is for you to take my tragic story to heart and learn from it. You DO NOT have to end up like me!"

The following are my best advice and opinions as a non-professional expert based on my personal life experiences with lawyers and the justice system. These are the things I wish I would have known before making the decision on whether or not to pursue legal action in this matter.

In other words, here's how NOT to get screwed like I did!

☐ **Think and research extremely hard before deciding to take legal action:**
There is a lot that can be learned from what happened in my tragic true story. When the defamation occurred in March and June of 2016, I felt so harassed and violated that I couldn't wait to get started with legal action. I wanted Lisa Vipperman to pay for what she did and I wanted it to happen, yesterday! I also felt that a lawsuit could stop the spread of defamatory info about me which threatened my reputation as a professional advocate for children, and also threatened my personal safety.

Now, looking back, we can all see what a huge, huge mistake that was. The defamation I endured had a two year statute of limitations during which I could potentially file a lawsuit; meaning I had until spring of 2018 to carefully explore ALL my options.

In retrospect, I should have talked to as many different lawyers as humanly possible before deciding on any one person to hire. As you know, I hired Brian right away because I knew him for many years and believed I could trust him. Had I taken the time to talk to 10-20 different lawyers, I might have learned some of the things that I felt Brian failed to tell me. I could have taken the time to do my own research on defamation cases via reading library books or looking up cases online. Also, by taking more time and not reacting quickly, I might have come up with feasible alternatives besides choosing legal action.

I also should have checked Brian's lawyer profile online (on avvo.com) to see if he truly had any significant experience in defamation cases. In other words, I should NOT have placed all my trust on him just because I had known him for six plus years and we had a friendly relationship. Yes he'd helped me regarding an employment law matter. But defamation is totally different, as I learned in the worst of ways!

Should you ever find yourself in a similar predicament, I recommend you think and research extremely hard before deciding to venture down this unpredictable path. Unless you are rich and famous, you should consider a lawsuit to be a windy road with signage stating: "VISIBILITY UNCLEAR AHEAD: PROCEED AT YOUR OWN RISK!"

⁇ A lawsuit is an assault upon you just as much as upon the person(s) you are suing

As recently noted, I filed a lawsuit to teach Lisa Vipperman a lesson and to restore my harmed reputation. Little did I realize that in declaring war on Vipperman, I was also declaring war on myself! I had no idea as to the true financial costs of legal action; the tremendous distress of depositions; the motions your opponent's lawyer can file or the claims they can level against you.

Beyond just Vipperman, I had to endure her attorney's insinuations that I was a strange, inappropriate grown up who was up to no good with those kids. Vipperman's lawyers tried to make these points over and over again in every motion that was filed and argued in court. In doing so, they added plenty of insult to the initial injury. So often during this lawsuit, I felt as though I WAS THE ONE BEING SUED!!!

I had no idea the courts would allow Vipperman's lawyers to use unrelated info such as the May 2016 alcohol incident against me in this lawsuit. I was NOT at fault, had done nothing wrong and was never questioned let alone charged by police in the teenagers' naughty stunt! Furthermore, the fluke occurrence had NOTHING to do with the defamation committed by Vipperman against me. Yet her lawyers tried to make sure it was one of the strongest points in each of their motions to the court. And according to the rules of a lawsuit, it was perfectly OK for them to do so!

It was good to find out at the end that the appellate judges eventually didn't focus on all those irrelevant discussions promoted by the defense lawyers – they simply focused on the fact that we were not able to show clear evidence of malice. But all those irrelevant discussions do have an impact on you. And if the case was allowed to go to a jury trial, such irrelevant information could have negatively impacted some of the jurors.

I was also taken by great surprise when Vipperman's lawyer filed the motion to compel a forensic examination of my communication devices; as well as the subsequent discovery requests seeking unlimited access to documents from every employer or organization I have ever been associated with! Though my lawyer made efforts to counter these attacks, I had no clue that the lawyer of the person you are suing can hassle you with demands for so much irrelevant information.

There's a saying that all is fair in love and war. It seems the same applies to a lawsuit. Be forewarned it could be as awful or worse on you as it will be on the person(s) you are suing!

▢ Filing a lawsuit does NOT guarantee that you will get your day in court

Herein lies perhaps the hardest kick in the pants of all. Aside from early concerns about Vipperman's lawyers and Anti-SLAPP, I never knew there was a thing called summary judgment floating around.

Amanda's grandmother – still bravely battling cancer today – was astounded to learn that my case had been dismissed in July 2018. "A jury would've likely seen this for how it was retaliation by Vipperman against you, Sumi!" my close friend had stated to me. "I thought if you filed a lawsuit that meant you would *get* to go to court in front of a jury. I never realized that it can just be dismissed like this."

And obviously, neither did I. I agree that if the facts of this case were presented to a jury, they would most likely have decided in my favor. However, I now know there are tough hurdles to overcome long before that can ever happen. Had I known of summary judgment or what's needed to survive it, I think that I could've prevailed. The lawsuit in my true story was one of defamation. I'm willing to bet other types of lawsuits also have difficult hurdles. The point to remember is that your day in court is NOT guaranteed!

⬜ Many Lawyers... in my opinion and from my experience...just simply cannot be trusted

Q: How does an attorney sleep?
A: First he lies on one side, then he lies on the other.
Q: How many lawyer jokes are there?
A: Only three. The rest are true stories.

I found the above quotes online when I did a search for "lawyer jokes" in July 2018. There are dozens of funny ones out there. What isn't so funny is the sad, hidden truth that far too many of these contain. It is apparent that many people have felt preyed upon by their lawyers. From my years of dealing with lawyers, and from what I have read about other situations, I believe that many cannot be trusted.

If you were to meet Brian Niemczyk, you would probably find him to be a very likeable, gentle, soft spoken person. That was certainly the image that won me over way back in 2010. As mentioned earlier, Brian proved helpful in the role he played in my employment law ordeal. Over the years, we had kept in touch and I met him for lunch on several occasions. It was typically Brian who had initiated the friendly encounters. He seemed interested in both my personal and professional life. He in turn shared about his professional life and a lot about his children as well.

In the beginning of this lawsuit, Brian went a step further and praised my father and me for how much he claimed that we already knew (as lay people) about the law. He voiced his encouragement for me to consider attending law school now in my early 40s - even citing the case of a fellow colleague of his who just became a lawyer at the age of 60 - as an example for me that it's never too late to choose a career in the legal world and to prosper at it.

Looking back now I believe that I had misunderstood these gestures by Brian as signs of friendship in a genuine manner. On the contrary, I now feel that I was being set up for the day I might once again need legal aid. His acting like my friend through the years made me feel a strong bond and a great sense of trust. When I found myself in peril in 2016, I immediately knew who to call. Rather than take time to research all options, I hired my friend on the spot. I felt lucky and ahead of the game that I knew a great lawyer right off the bat.

Not only did I fully believe Brian that I had a winnable case and that he was equipped to handle defamation, but I never thought he could make critical errors or omissions like the way I believe he did and not care. I simply didn't think that I would ever lose trust in the soft spoken 'nice guy' and family man I knew for 6-8 years. He was my ally and good friend. He knew my income was small, that my dad was retired and that we didn't have money to burn! I struggle to see how he sleeps at night after profiting from our demise.

Setting aside the fortune we wasted on a horribly handled case, my experience with Brian on this case also took away the basic trust I had in the goodness of all people, particularly lawyers! If we can't trust a Brian Niemczyk in the legal world, then who exactly can we rely on?!

My answer to that question folks is YOU SHOULD RELY ON NO LAWYER, as far as possible. If there's one thing you can get from reading this book, it's that you DO NOT want to end up like me! Every day since the July 2018 decision, I've kicked myself over how I could have fallen for it all. Looking back now it's so easy to see what I wasn't able to then. Ironically, in retrospect, my involvement in this case has taught me more about the law and the legal world than I had ever wanted to know!

My advice is for you to take my tragic story to heart and learn from it. You DO NOT have to end up like me! Even if you do choose a lawyer and decide to take legal action, always keep your guard up and don't forget what they might be capable of. THEY ARE NEVER, EVER, EVER YOUR FRIEND!!!

There is one thing that bothered me after the fact. In his email of April 5, 2016, Brian had mentioned that his management did not want to go with the contingency approach that I had asked for because they had concerns about actually collecting any judgment that I might obtain against the defendant. He also stated that "we generally only take cases on a contingency when we are very sure of our ability to actually collect the money needed to pay our fees if we win." I understood that since at that time the defendant was not being supported by the hotel's insurance.

When we knew that the insurance company had decided to support her on this, then why didn't Brian think of going back to a contingency contract because with the insurance company involved there will be no concerns about collecting any judgment? I admit that I had not thought of that myself at the time – I take that responsibility. But

Brian knew our financial concerns very well and he knew that I had asked for a contingency approach – so why didn't he think of it? I am not blaming anyone for this, but I do feel that if Brian was a friend, like I thought he was, I wish he had thought of that. That would have made me feel like he really cared.

There is another example when I felt he did not act like a trusted friend that I thought he was. One of the lawyers we met with after the case was over, had produced a list of all Brian's cases since around 2006. I didn't even know that there was a way to get something like this. There were 481 cases listed. If you take a quick look at it, you can easily see that the vast majority of those were "eviction" related. Only 32 of the 481 were identified as "civil/other/misc". I didn't take the time to go through each of these cases to find out how many of the 32 were defamation cases.

This may not be the best way to analyze his experience, but I must say that once I looked at that list, I certainly felt that I made a mistake sticking with Brian for this case. I again felt that I made the mistake of thinking of him as a friend and trusting him wholeheartedly when he indicated that he had experience in defamation cases. I believe that my thinking of him as a friend had blinded me. That is why my advice is not to think of your lawyer as a friend.

Do thorough research before deciding which one to go with, including checking to see if the lawyer has ever been disciplined or even considered for discipline. You can easily do this online, along with searching former clients' reviews about the lawyer you are considering.

When looking for malpractice attorneys in Minneapolis, I performed an online search on a particular lawyer's name along with the word "discipline," and I came upon records of alleged misconduct committed by that attorney which was considered for possible discipline! In that case the attorney was eventually cleared and not officially disciplined, but I still knew that there had been an allegation of misconduct made against him.

The following link: http://lprb.mncourts.gov/LawyerSearch/Pages/default.aspx, allows you to look up any lawyer in Minnesota and check his or her disciplinary history. I'm guessing every state has a similar link.

Still, a confirmed record of discipline most often will not exist to warn you in advance of a lawyer you wouldn't want to hire. Your best bet is to do thorough research, trust your instincts and get many, many second opinions.

IF AT ALL HUMANLY POSSIBLE DO NOT DEAL WITH A
LAWYER AT ALL!!!!!

⍰ Watch out for overconfidence and negative comments towards other lawyers

As you know well, my lawyer's approach (as per my observations) consisted of chronic statements that came across to me as overconfidence and undermining the abilities of the other lawyers. Never so was the approach of my second attorney Barbara, who had handled my appeal of the summary judgment decision.

I firmly believe that overconfidence and negative comments about the opposing lawyers are red flag warnings. If you look at how Barbara prepared me for the appeal, she always said we were fighting an uphill battle and that nothing was guaranteed. She also expressed her belief that the arguments made by lawyers on both sides of this battle were good, unlike Brian who constantly said that the other side's lawyers were making errors or taking a wrong approach.

Though many lawyers cannot be trusted, I say that the ones with overconfidence and negative comments for opposing counsel should be considered concerning. If something seems too good to be true, then it probably is. Even when talking with different malpractice attorneys following the loss of my case, we felt that ALL of them appeared more experienced and knowledgeable with hourly rates significantly less than the rate that we had to pay for my lawyer... and to lose my case long before trial! This proved to me again that I should have taken more time before deciding on which lawyer to go with for my lawsuit.

⬜ Do not judge a judge's behavior

This was a lesson I had originally learned during my unemployment benefits hearing back in the summer of 2010. Sadly, it was reinforced again in this defamation lawsuit in April 2018.

At the earlier unemployment hearing - detailed in my third book about workplace bullying - the judge had grilled me with questions and even made statements indicating he could understand my ex-employer's position on the issues. Yet, as it turned out, that same judge eventually ruled in my favor!

And as we saw in the appeal hearing of the summary judgment decision, the judges appeared to take Vipperman's lawyer to task and seriously question the lower court's decision to grant summary judgment in Vipperman's favor. It was enough to fool my lawyer Brian into fully believing that I would likely prevail. But as we saw in July 2018, I did not win in the second case.

If you should ever find yourself involved in legal action, it is wise not to judge a judge's behavior. I can tell you from my real life experiences, their behaviors may not match with their rulings!

⁇ Lawsuits are horrendously expensive

Unless you are a ridiculously lucky individual like Lisa Vipperman, most lawsuits are going to be horrendously expensive. Many law firms will not take a case on a much preferred contingency arrangement – meaning where you only pay once your lawyer has won a settlement and then your lawyer gets a portion of your settlement. Brian's firm of Hellmuth & Johnson refused the contingency option to us right from the start. That immediately should have tipped me off that they didn't believe I had a great shot of prospering in this matter, even though in words they had told me that I had a 'good claim.'

A contingency arrangement also ensures that your attorney will put in his or her finest efforts, as they will NOT be getting paid unless YOU are getting paid! But since the goal of most law firms is to pocket their clients' money, many may not agree to a contingency option which would benefit the client. Make no mistake about it, they are looking out for themselves and seeking to prosper from your misfortune!

There may of course be exceptions to this rule, such as if you have overwhelming, slam dunk evidence against your opponent; if you were physically injured in an accident; or perhaps if it is a wrongful death lawsuit. The contingency option seems to become more likely under those circumstances. If you are not a celebrity or do not have a special connection with someone at a law firm, you should expect to pay your legal fees out of pocket... just as we did.

Along with the costs and expenses involved in each step of the lawsuit (along with having to pay the other side's expenses if you lose a motion like the summary judgment), you will be billed for every text, email or single word spoken with your attorney. That's the nature of this ugly business which benefits all of the law firms.

Following my experience with the legal system, I have come to conclude that lawyers and lawsuits are primarily for the wealthy and privileged. Had my father and I received a better estimate of the *actual* costs and expenses involved, I can almost guarantee that I WOULD NOT HAVE FILED THIS LAWSUIT!!!!!!

☑ **Lawyers for businesses or companies will work harder for their client than your attorney will work for you**

Unless you are blessed with fighting a case on a preferred contingency basis, lawyers for businesses or companies will work harder for their client than your attorney will work for you.

This point was made crystal clear in my tragic true story. Vipperman's legal team worked for the hotel's insurance company. They were hired by the insurance company and were accountable to the insurance company for prevailing in this matter. They needed to do an excellent job so the insurance company will continue to come to them for their other cases. As a result, they were aggressive advocates for their client Lisa Vipperman and gave her a commendable defense, all free of charge.

As you witnessed, Brian and his law firm felt no similar sense of accountability to me, whatsoever. That was a stunning difference between the quality of representation that Vipperman received compared to what I received. On the contrary, Brian's firm didn't even pacify us with a couple thousand dollars as a show of appreciation towards one of their most committed clients who had given them close to **ONE HUNDRED GRAND**... only to lose much before trial!

Without a contingency arrangement in place, my lawyer Brian was going to be paid a whole lot of money... regardless of his actual performance. And unlike Vipperman's lawyers' commitment to the insurance company, Brian and his firm couldn't have cared less how I felt about the job Brian had done, after the matter concluded. I had certainly not taken this difference of approach into consideration before deciding to file the lawsuit.

After all, at the time I decided to file, I was expecting to sue Lisa Vipperman as an individual. I was blindsided by the hotel's decision to become involved in the matter! But once they did, I believe that they gave Vipperman far better representation than Brian and his firm gave to me.

Be forewarned in a lawsuit, to expect the unexpected. Nothing is guaranteed and risk is involved every step of the way! Even Vipperman herself - who got lucky this time – might not be quite so fortunate the next time around.

Barring a contingency arrangement, your attorney is just there to get paid. A business or company's lawyer will have a much bigger stake in the game!

☑ It is extremely difficult to successfully sue a lawyer for malpractice

As described in Chapter 18, it is extremely difficult to successfully sue a lawyer for malpractice. What I understood is that barring blatant misconduct that is wild and outrageous, most claims such as mine against Brian will likely get thrown out of court in the summary judgment phase. As we saw with Brian's boss Chad Johnson at Hellmuth & Johnson, the lawyers are keenly aware of their powerful advantage over us.

Besides the summary judgment reality, most people who need to sue a lawyer already suffered a loss and don't have the means to afford to pay an expert to strengthen their case. Unless you have slam dunk evidence against your former attorney, few if any malpractice lawyers will take your case on a contingency basis.

It seems to me that prevailing in the legal system is often based on how much money you have to play with. It is hence, again, my reason for believing that lawsuits are for the wealthy and privileged. Folks like us ought to try and avoid them if at all humanly possible!

This lesson also reiterates the importance of NOT poorly choosing a lawyer should you decide that you *have* to take legal action. If you make a bad choice as I feel that I did, you're going to be stuck with the consequences.

There's no remedy available after the fact (not even with the Lawyers Professional Responsibility

Board), as my case illustrates in the harshest of ways!!!!!!

▢ A defamer may have legal privileges if they slander your name from their place of work or if they slander you to people in law enforcement

Herein are two of the hardest lessons which came my way in this lawsuit.

Lisa Vipperman might as well go ahead and purchase a lottery ticket, because if she didn't study the law one can only marvel at how undeservingly fortunate she was in this predicament. As I see it, she was damn lucky to have slandered my name from her place of work and also to persons in law enforcement!

As we learned in the worst of ways, both of these methods of operation brought tremendous advantages to my defamer. Because the defamation occurred from her place of work and in the course of her supposed 'job duties,' Vipperman became eligible to have her legal expenses covered by the hotel's insurance company.

As explained previously, this was a huge factor which enabled her to file expensive motions (including summary judgment and motion to compel) and ultimately prevail against me. Most likely, she would not have been able to do so if she had been defending herself with a private attorney. And of course because she defamed me to persons in law enforcement, we also needed clear evidence of malice to survive summary judgment.

Not to say that the latter could not have been overcome if, as per my understanding, I'd had a more experienced attorney with regards to defamation... one who'd have known that it was necessary to show adequate evidence of malice to overcome the qualified privilege and survive summary judgment. Regardless, it might have been a whole different story if Vipperman had committed slander out in the community instead of from work and to regular citizens rather than to the police.

Be forewarned, legal privileges may exist under certain circumstances for those who seek out to commit defamation!

EPILOGUE

"I hope to use this true story as an example of how one can fight back diligently, aggressively, ethically, honestly and without resorting to violence."

Many people are of the belief that everything bad in our lives happens for a reason. I am not one of those people. However, I do believe that it is up to each one of us - whenever possible - to try and derive something positive from the terrible ills which befall us.

This true story is an excellent example. In this book, I have discussed at length the reasons why I feel I was a victim of Vipperman, of my attorney, and of the justice system. The ending was obviously not what I would have preferred as a positive outcome! Regardless, this story has immeasurable value now in teaching and assisting others.

This book provides a rare inside look into lawyers, lawsuits and the justice system. It informs readers of the racism still plaguing our country today, and teaches fellow minorities of the dangers we can face and how to combat them. It shows how we may learn from our failures more than if we had simply prevailed. It reminds us of the value in doing the right thing even if we don't win every time. I hope to use this true story as an example of how one can fight back diligently, aggressively, ethically, honestly and without resorting to violence.

I acknowledge my legal battle would not have been possible without the tremendous emotional and financial support of my parents, first and foremost.

I also express my deepest appreciation for all the people who told the truth courageously and stood up for me in the course of this lengthy ordeal.

They include: Amanda's grandmother, Amanda's father, Amanda, Kelsey's mother Jennifer, Kelsey, Kelsey's friend and her mother, Mark and his mother. Also, Barbara, the attorney who handled my appeal, Officer Ryan Franz and Deerwood Police Chief Mark Taylor. Some endured personal stress and hardship as a result of becoming involved in my legal battle. I did not win in court as I hoped. Still, I fought the good fight with their help and will always be grateful for all their support!!!

I regret going into this lawsuit as misinformed as I was. However, I do not regret taking a stand for myself and keeping wrongdoers in check! Is legal action the proper solution to a conflict? That decision can only be yours...

The purpose of my book was to tell you THE TRUTH and my own thoughts and feelings about what happened, why and what all can be involved in real life situations like these!!!

About the Author

Author and Speaker Sumi Mukherjee writes non-fiction books based on real life stories and speaks to audiences about the messages contained in his books. His focus is on bringing about positive changes in our society, with specific emphasis on racial equality, prevention of bullying and child sexual abuse. Since October 2011, Sumi has been speaking to hundreds of people around the country so others can benefit from his stories. Sumi has spoken to teachers, counselors, administrators, social workers, school psychologists, mental health professionals, family members, caregivers, service providers, law enforcement professionals, students, parents, and the general audience. He has spoken at schools, colleges, religious organizations, bullying prevention conferences, other professional conferences (including School Social Workers Association conferences, School Psychologists Association Conference, Counseling Association Conferences, State Psychological Association Conferences), child abuse prevention conferences, domestic violence/sexual abuse/mental health awareness events. Sumi has spoken extensively all over the United States as well as in Canada. Sumi was born in Calgary, Canada, and grew up in Minneapolis, USA. For more information please visit his website at www.authorsumi.com

Made in USA - Kendallville, IN
1213201_9781946072757
12.15.2020 0824